MUMBAI

Travel Guide 2025

Top Destinations, Vibrant Culture, and Local Insights for Exploring India's City of Dreams

Deborah Martha

No part of this publication may be reproduced, stored or transmitted in any form or by any means, electronic, mechanical, photocopying, recording, scanning, or otherwise without written permission from the publisher.

It is illegal to copy this book, post it to a website, or distribute it by any other means without permission.

Copyright © 2024 Deborah Martha
All rights reserved.

Table of Content

INTRODUCTION 6

    Welcome to Mumbai: An Overview of the City of Dreams 7

    Why Visit Mumbai in 2025: Trends, Events, and Travel Highlights 10

    Essential Travel Tips: When to Go, What to Expect, and Cultural Etiquette 14

    Visa Requirements 18

Getting to Know Mumbai 22

    A Brief History of Mumbai 22

    Culture and People: Embracing Mumbai's Melting Pot of Traditions 23

    Quick Facts: Language, Currency, and Local Customs 24

    Navigating the City: Transportation Options and Tips for Getting Around 25

Iconic Landmarks of Mumbai 27

    The Gateway of India: Historical Significance and Visitor Tips 27

    Chhatrapati Shivaji Maharaj Terminus: A UNESCO Heritage Marvel 28

    Marine Drive and the Queen's Necklace: Coastal Beauty and Evening Walks 29

    Haji Ali Dargah: Pilgrimage Site and Architectural Wonder 30

    Siddhivinayak Temple: Spiritual Significance and Local Devotion 31

Exploring Mumbai's Neighborhoods 32

    Colaba: Shopping, Dining, and Famous Sights 33

    Fort and Kala Ghoda: Art, Architecture, and Cafés 34

    Bandra: The Celebrity Hub, Street Art, and Trendy Spots 34

    Juhu and Versova: Beaches, Bollywood, and Food Culture 35

    Dharavi: Understanding Asia's Largest Slum with Ethical Tours 37

MUMBAI TRAVEL GUIDE 2025

Mumbai's Cultural Scene 38
- Bollywood and Beyond 38
- Art and Museums 39
- Traditional Festivals: Ganesh Chaturthi, Diwali, and Other Celebrations 40
- Music and Dance: Classical, Contemporary, and Street Performances 41

Culinary Journey Through Mumbai 43
- An Introduction to Mumbai Cuisine 43
- Must-Try Dishes: Vada Pav, Pav Bhaji, Bhel Puri, Pani Puri, and More 44
- Street Food Hotspots: Khau Gallis, Chowpatty Beach, and Local Markets 45
- Fine Dining and Iconic Restaurants 46
- Food Tours and Cooking Classes 47

Shopping and Markets 48
- Street Markets: Colaba Causeway, Fashion Street, and Crawford Market 48
- Local Art and Crafts: Souvenirs and Handicrafts to Take Home 49
- High-End Malls and Boutiques 50
- Tips for Bargaining and Navigating Mumbai's Markets 51
- Practical Tips 52

Nightlife and Entertainment 56
- Popular Nightclubs, Bars, and Lounges 56
- Rooftop Bars and Sea-Facing Venues 57
- Cultural Performances and Theatres 57
- Tips for Staying Safe While Enjoying Mumbai's Nightlife 58

Mumbai's Spiritual and Religious Sites 60
- Temples of Mumbai 60
- Churches and Cathedrals 61
- Mosques and Shrines 62

MUMBAI TRAVEL GUIDE 2025

    Multi-Faith Harmony: Experiencing Mumbai's Religious Diversity 62

    Practical Tips and Travel Guide Tips 63

Family-Friendly Activities 67

    Kid-Friendly Attractions 67

    Family Beaches and Picnic Spots 68

    Practical Tips and Travel Guide Tips 71

Mumbai for the Adventurous Traveler 75

    Urban Exploring: Offbeat Locations, Graffiti Spots, and Unique Finds 75

    Trekking Trails: Kanheri Caves, Yeoor Hills, and Nearby Destinations 76

    Exploring the Local Night Markets and Late-Night Food Scenes 78

Practical Travel Information 80

    Travel Essentials: Visa, Currency Exchange, and Mobile Connectivity 80

    Staying Safe in Mumbai: Tips on Health, Safety, and Avoiding Scams 84

    Navigating Medical Services and Pharmacies 86

Insider Tips and Local Insights 89

    Mumbai Through a Local's Eyes: Authentic Experiences and Hidden Gems 89

    Best Photo Spots: Capturing Mumbai's Scenic and Vibrant Moments 90

    Timing Your Visit: When to Avoid Crowds, Best Times for Attractions 92

Conclusion 94

    Useful Contacts: Emergency Numbers, Consulates, and Travel Agencies 94

    Mumbai by Season: Weather Guide and Packing Tips 96

MUMBAI TRAVEL GUIDE 2025

INTRODUCTION

Welcome to Mumbai, a city that never sleeps, where modern ambitions and deep-rooted traditions converge to create one of the world's most exhilarating destinations. Known as India's "City of Dreams," Mumbai stands as a vibrant metropolis, constantly evolving yet firmly anchored in its cultural legacy. From its iconic waterfront Gateway of India to the bustling street markets, from Bollywood glitz to historic colonial architecture, Mumbai offers an experience as diverse as the people who call it home.

As the financial and entertainment capital of India, Mumbai draws millions of visitors each year—not only for its landmarks but for the immersive local experiences that capture the heart and soul of the city. In 2025, Mumbai continues to expand its offerings with new attractions, revitalized historical sites, and enhanced traveler amenities. This guide is crafted to help you explore the best of Mumbai, whether you're a first-time visitor or a returning traveler eager to uncover the city's latest treasures.

In the following chapters, we'll take you through Mumbai's top destinations, local customs, and hidden gems, offering practical travel tips along the way. You'll get insights into must-see landmarks, culinary delights, lively neighborhoods, and seasonal festivals, as well as guidance on navigating Mumbai's dynamic streets. Beyond the well-known sights, you'll discover how to engage with the city's vibrant culture—from savoring local street food to experiencing the magic of a Bollywood film, or simply unwinding by the Arabian Sea at sunset.

So, pack your bags, bring your sense of adventure, and prepare to be captivated by the allure of Mumbai. Your journey to the heart of India's most dynamic city begins here.

Welcome to Mumbai: An Overview of the City of Dreams

Mumbai is a city where every corner pulses with energy and ambition, a place that has grown from its roots as a group of fishing islands to become the thriving economic and cultural capital of India. Known as the "City of Dreams," it's where millions arrive daily—some with dreams of fortune, others in search of new opportunities, and many simply to immerse themselves in its unmatched vibrancy. Here, the future is built upon a foundation of rich history, layered with traditions that stretch back centuries, yet deeply intertwined with the global culture of today.

A walk through Mumbai is an immersion in contrasts: you'll find ancient temples beside ultra-modern skyscrapers, colonial architecture sharing the skyline with Bollywood film studios, and bustling street vendors just steps away from high-end designer boutiques. The city embodies a remarkable resilience and resourcefulness, thriving despite its challenges and evolving constantly to meet the needs of its ever-growing population. This diverse dynamism is part of what gives Mumbai its unique character—an urban tapestry woven with the dreams and cultures of people from every corner of India and beyond.

Mumbai is divided into various neighborhoods, each with its own distinct personality and history. South Mumbai is home to the iconic Gateway of India, Chhatrapati Shivaji Maharaj Terminus, and many architectural gems from the British Raj. Colaba

MUMBAI TRAVEL GUIDE 2025

and Fort are the city's historic heart, brimming with colonial-era buildings, art galleries, and local markets. Bandra is where Mumbai's modern glamour shines; it's a trendy district known for its cafés, sea-facing promenades, and as the residence of many

Bollywood stars. Juhu, famous for its beach and lively atmosphere, offers a peek into local life and is a popular spot to sample Mumbai's beloved street foods.

One of the highlights of Mumbai is its cuisine, which offers everything from traditional Marathi dishes to innovative fusion flavors inspired by its multicultural population. Street food is an essential part of the city's identity. Here, you'll find locals and visitors alike enjoying vada pav (Mumbai's take on a spicy potato slider), bhel puri, pav bhaji, and an endless variety of chaat. For food lovers, Mumbai's khau gallis (food streets) are a must-visit, with tempting aromas and vibrant dishes served from bustling food stalls.

Beyond its famous landmarks and culinary delights, Mumbai's spirit lies in its people. Known for their resilience and warmth, Mumbaikars embody the city's boundless energy. Whether during the monsoon season, when rains bring the city to a temporary standstill, or in the scorching heat of summer, they continue to work, create, and celebrate life with unwavering determination. Visitors often speak of the unique blend of grit and kindness they encounter here, a defining trait of Mumbai's character.

Mumbai's art and culture scene is equally impressive, from the galleries of Kala Ghoda to the colorful street art in Bandra's back alleys. Bollywood, India's prolific film industry, calls Mumbai home, making it the epicenter of the nation's entertainment. Visitors can catch glimpses of film shoots around the city or even book a tour of a Bollywood studio to see firsthand how the magic unfolds.

For the traveler, Mumbai can be both exhilarating and overwhelming. Its fast-paced way of life, crowded streets, and round-the-clock activity may require some adjustment, but it's all part of the adventure. Once you've embraced the rhythm, Mumbai reveals itself to be not only a city of dreams but also a city of endless discovery. It offers layers of history, culture, and modern-day allure that few other places can match.

Visiting Mumbai in 2025 brings new and exciting possibilities, as the city continues to innovate and develop. From newly opened museums to restored heritage sites and expanded public spaces, there's always something fresh to experience. Whether you're here for the architectural splendor, the cinematic magic, or simply to soak in the atmosphere, Mumbai invites you to join in its journey.

MUMBAI TRAVEL GUIDE 2025

This guide is your companion to explore Mumbai's sights, neighborhoods, flavors, and stories. It's crafted to help you see beyond the obvious, navigate the challenges, and embrace the vibrant diversity that defines this extraordinary city. So, step into the heart of Mumbai and get ready to experience the city of dreams like never before.

Why Visit Mumbai in 2025: Trends, Events, and Travel Highlights

In 2025, Mumbai offers an extraordinary experience for travelers, blending new and timeless attractions with a lineup of fresh trends and events that make it one of the most exciting destinations in Asia. Known as the "City of Dreams," Mumbai continues to evolve while celebrating its unique heritage. From groundbreaking architectural developments to a packed calendar of events, Mumbai is a cultural and urban marvel that has something for every traveler. Here's why visiting Mumbai in 2025 promises an unforgettable journey.

1. Cultural Renaissance and Urban Developments

Mumbai is currently in the midst of an urban renaissance, with ambitious projects designed to enhance both the city's landscape and the quality of life for its residents and visitors. In 2025, the iconic Marine Drive promenade has been upgraded with eco-friendly features, art installations, and expanded seating areas, offering a modernized yet nostalgic view of Mumbai's coastline. Several new public spaces have also opened, including the coastal park along the Mumbai Trans-Harbor Link, where you can enjoy panoramic views of the city's skyline while surrounded by greenery.

The recent restoration of heritage sites like the Chhatrapati Shivaji Maharaj Terminus and the Elephanta Caves ensures that these cultural landmarks shine even brighter for visitors, with guided tours that offer deeper insights into their history and significance. Art lovers will find the Kala Ghoda Art Precinct bustling with creative energy, as galleries introduce new exhibits and installations, highlighting contemporary Indian art and the city's storied cultural history.

2. A Thriving Food Scene and Culinary Experiences

MUMBAI TRAVEL GUIDE 2025

Mumbai's culinary scene in 2025 is vibrant and continues to embrace innovative trends, making it a hotspot for food enthusiasts. Traditional flavors meet creative fusions, with a rise in "farm-to-table" dining and sustainable, locally-sourced cuisine. Restaurants such as Bombay Canteen and Masque are pushing culinary boundaries, focusing on regional ingredients that celebrate India's vast biodiversity.

Street food is also experiencing a fresh wave of popularity, with special events dedicated to Mumbai's beloved dishes. In 2025, the city hosts the "Mumbai Street Food Festival," a celebration of flavors that draws locals and tourists alike to indulge in classic bites such as vada pav, pav bhaji, and bhel puri, prepared by some of the city's most talented street vendors. This year, expect a twist on traditional flavors as chefs introduce new ingredients and cooking techniques that retain the authenticity of these iconic snacks while offering something entirely unique.

For the health-conscious traveler, new organic cafés and plant-based restaurants are popping up throughout neighborhoods like Bandra and Lower Parel, where visitors can enjoy a fresh take on Indian classics with a focus on wellness and sustainability. In 2025, Mumbai's food culture is as rich and varied as its population, offering a culinary journey that's sure to captivate any palate.

3. Bollywood Fever: Entertainment and Film Industry Highlights

Bollywood, the heart of India's film industry, is bigger than ever in 2025. Visitors can immerse themselves in the magic of Indian cinema through studio tours, movie-themed events, and exclusive screenings. New Bollywood-themed attractions and tours provide behind-the-scenes glimpses into how the magic of cinema is made, while the annual Mumbai Film Festival continues to gain global recognition, drawing filmmakers, actors, and cinephiles from around the world.

For travelers fascinated by Bollywood's glitz and glamour, now is the perfect time to visit. The industry is marking milestones this year with retrospectives on legendary films, interactive exhibits, and opportunities to catch live filming around the city. Studios have also introduced workshops where visitors can learn about Bollywood dance, costume design, and even scriptwriting. Bollywood isn't just a genre of film here; it's a way of life, and Mumbai invites you to step into this vibrant world.

4. Festivals and Events: An Endless Calendar of Celebrations

Mumbai's events calendar is packed with celebrations, festivals, and cultural showcases that highlight the city's vibrant spirit. In 2025, the city hosts an array of festivals, each adding a layer of excitement and cultural immersion for visitors. From the grand Ganesh Chaturthi festivities, where intricately designed Ganesh idols are carried through the streets before a ceremonial immersion, to the springtime Holi Festival, known for its colorful revelry, Mumbai's celebrations are an experience like no other.

New Year's Eve and Diwali are marked with massive fireworks displays along Marine Drive, offering a stunning backdrop against the Arabian Sea. In January, the Kala Ghoda Arts Festival transforms the city into an open-air gallery, with art installations, street performances, and workshops attracting artists and audiences from across the globe. Another major event is the Mumbai Marathon, which brings together participants from around the world, showcasing Mumbai's community spirit and iconic cityscape.

For travelers interested in music, the Magnetic Fields Festival in early spring combines electronic and traditional Indian music, providing an immersive experience with both live and digital performances at some of the city's best venues. Mumbai in 2025 is more than a destination—it's a year-round celebration of art, music, and community.

5. Sustainable and Responsible Tourism

In response to global calls for sustainable tourism, Mumbai is making strides toward more eco-friendly travel options and environmentally conscious practices. The city's green initiatives, such as solar-powered public transportation, new eco-parks, and beach clean-ups, have gained momentum in 2025, and travelers are encouraged to participate. Programs like the "Adopt-a-Beach" initiative allow visitors to help maintain the beauty of Juhu and Versova beaches, contributing to Mumbai's sustainability goals.

Accommodations and tour operators are increasingly prioritizing eco-friendly practices, offering options that reduce carbon footprints without sacrificing comfort. Mumbai's focus on responsible tourism means travelers can enjoy the city with a sense of stewardship, contributing to a positive impact while they explore. Many tours now offer low-impact experiences, from walking tours of heritage areas to eco-cruises along the Arabian Sea, which allow travelers to witness the beauty of the city without contributing to overcrowding or pollution.

6. Adventure and Exploration

For the adventurous traveler, Mumbai offers unique explorations and outdoor activities that add a thrill to the urban experience. In 2025, Mumbai's outdoor offerings are expanding with guided coastal treks, nature trails, and new water sports along the Arabian Sea. Popular trails like the Sanjay Gandhi National Park trek provide an escape into nature right within the city's boundaries, with guided tours offering insights into the local flora, fauna, and history.

The newly established zipline experience across Gorai Creek has become a highlight, giving adrenaline seekers a chance to glide above the water and catch panoramic views of Mumbai's outskirts. For those interested in underwater adventures, new diving and snorkeling options near Marine Drive allow travelers to explore the Arabian Sea's marine life while enjoying the city's unique coastal landscape.

Why Now is the Time to Visit Mumbai

Mumbai in 2025 is more than a bustling metropolis—it's a city committed to redefining urban life through creativity, resilience, and community engagement. Whether you're drawn by its storied history, its booming arts and culture, or simply the promise of new adventures, Mumbai welcomes travelers with open arms and an endless list of experiences. Now is the time to visit this ever-evolving city, to witness its continued transformation and to be part of its journey as it embraces both tradition and innovation.

As you explore Mumbai, you'll find yourself caught up in its infectious energy, captivated by the warmth of its people, and surprised by its blend of old and new. With so much to see and experience, Mumbai in 2025 promises to be a destination that not only meets but exceeds your expectations, leaving you with memories and stories to cherish for years to come.

Essential Travel Tips: When to Go, What to Expect, and Cultural Etiquette

Navigating Mumbai can be a wonderfully immersive experience, with its vibrant cityscapes, diverse traditions, and buzzing energy at every corner. Understanding the best time to visit, what to expect during your stay, and how to embrace cultural nuances can make your journey seamless and deeply rewarding. Here's a practical guide to help you plan your visit to Mumbai, ensuring a memorable experience while respecting local customs and practices.

When to Go: Choosing the Ideal Time to Visit Mumbai

Mumbai experiences three primary seasons: winter (November to February), summer (March to May), and monsoon (June to September). Each season offers a different take on the city, so choosing when to visit depends on what you hope to experience.

- Winter (November to February): This is widely considered the best time to visit Mumbai, with temperatures ranging from a comfortable 20°C to 30°C (68°F to 86°F). The humidity is lower, making it ideal for sightseeing and outdoor activities. This period also coincides with major festivals like Diwali (the festival of lights) and Christmas, when the city is alive with celebrations and decorations.

- Summer (March to May): Mumbai's summer is hot, with temperatures soaring up to 35°C (95°F) and high humidity levels, which can make sightseeing challenging. However, if you're interested in Mumbai's lively indoor scenes, such as cultural performances, museums, and bustling markets, this season can be an exciting time to explore the city's artistic side.

- Monsoon (June to September): Monsoon season transforms Mumbai, with heavy rain and occasional flooding. For some travelers, the monsoon is a unique draw, adding a romantic touch to the city's scenery. Popular spots like Marine Drive and Worli Sea Face take on an almost cinematic look with the mist and waves crashing against the shore. However, be prepared for transportation delays, and carry rain gear if you choose to visit during this time.

Overall, winter remains the most favorable time to visit, particularly if you want to make the most of Mumbai's outdoor attractions. However, the city's year-round energy ensures that there's always something to see and experience, no matter the season.

What to Expect: From Bustling Streets to Serene Hideaways

Mumbai is a city of contrasts and extremes, where fast-paced urban life coexists with quiet temples, historical neighborhoods, and serene coastal views. Here's what you can expect during your stay:

- Diverse Urban Landscapes: Mumbai's neighborhoods are as varied as its residents. South Mumbai, home to historical landmarks like the Gateway of India and the Chhatrapati Shivaji Maharaj Terminus, boasts grand colonial architecture. In contrast, the suburbs, including areas like Bandra and Juhu, have a modern, cosmopolitan feel, with trendy cafes, art galleries, and lively nightlife.

- Traffic and Transportation: Mumbai is known for its heavy traffic, particularly during rush hours. While the traffic may be overwhelming at first, the city's efficient public transport options, including local trains, buses, and auto-rickshaws, can help you navigate around. For added comfort, services like Uber and Ola provide convenient ways to get around, though you may need to plan ahead during peak times.

- **Warm Hospitality and Helpful Locals:** Mumbai's people, known locally as "Mumbaikars," are known for their resilience, friendliness, and willingness to help. Whether you're asking for directions or recommendations, locals are often eager to assist, sometimes even going out of their way to ensure you reach your destination. Many residents speak English, which makes communication relatively easy for international travelers.

- **Contrasts in Wealth and Social Conditions:** Mumbai's economic diversity is stark, with luxury high-rises standing side by side with densely populated slum areas. This contrast can be a thought-provoking aspect of your visit, offering insights into the city's complex social fabric. Respecting and understanding these differences can add depth to your experience, reminding you of the resilience and unity that define Mumbai.

Cultural Etiquette: How to Embrace Mumbai's Traditions Respectfully

Mumbai's diverse population brings together customs and practices from across India, making it a melting pot of traditions. Here are some key cultural etiquette tips to help you connect more authentically with the city and its people.

- **Dress Modestly:** While Mumbai is more liberal than other parts of India, dressing modestly is still recommended, especially when visiting temples, mosques, or other sacred sites. Men and women should avoid revealing clothing, as this can be seen as disrespectful in more traditional areas. Loose, breathable clothing is also practical given the city's warm climate.

- **Respect Sacred Spaces:** Mumbai is home to various religious sites, including Hindu temples, mosques, and churches. When entering these spaces, remove your shoes and dress modestly. In Hindu temples, it's customary to make a small offering, such as flowers, when visiting the deity. Photography is often restricted in sacred areas, so it's best to ask for permission if you're unsure.

- **Use the Right Hand:** In Indian culture, the right hand is considered auspicious, and is typically used for eating, giving, and receiving items. Using your left hand may be seen as disrespectful, particularly in traditional settings. When shaking hands, giving money, or exchanging items, try to use your right hand as a sign of respect.

- Negotiating Prices: Bargaining is common in Mumbai's local markets, and is often expected. Approach it with a friendly attitude, as locals appreciate good-natured negotiation. While larger stores and chains have fixed prices, street vendors and market stalls are generally open to negotiation, so don't be afraid to haggle, especially at places like Colaba Causeway and Crawford Market.

- Avoid Public Displays of Affection: Public displays of affection, such as kissing or hugging, are generally considered inappropriate in India. Holding hands or a quick embrace is usually acceptable, but more intimate gestures are best reserved for private spaces.

- Greetings and Personal Space: Indians commonly greet each other with a nod or a "namaste," where palms are pressed together as if in prayer. In more formal settings, a handshake is also acceptable. Personal space may be perceived differently in Mumbai, especially in crowded areas, but people are generally respectful of each other's space. Being mindful and polite in crowded spaces is appreciated.

Practical Advice for a Smooth Visit

To make the most of your trip, consider a few practical tips that can help you avoid unnecessary stress:

- Health and Hygiene: Carry hand sanitizer, as you may not always find facilities in every location. Tap water is not safe to drink in Mumbai, so rely on bottled or filtered water instead. In restaurants, check if the water is filtered before drinking.

- Local Sim Card and Internet Access: Staying connected in Mumbai is easy, with many hotels and cafes offering free Wi-Fi. For more reliable access, consider purchasing a local SIM card, which is affordable and provides data for navigation, communication, and staying up to date.

- Safety and Security: While Mumbai is considered safe for tourists, it's still essential to stay cautious, especially in crowded areas where pickpocketing can occur. Keep your belongings secure, avoid displaying valuables, and stay aware of your surroundings. Solo travelers, especially women, should exercise caution at night and stick to well-lit, busy areas.

- Currency and Payments: India's currency is the Indian Rupee (INR). While cash is essential for small transactions, digital payments are widely accepted, especially in larger establishments. Mobile payment apps such as Paytm and Google Pay are popular and convenient for travelers, making it easy to pay without carrying excessive cash.

Conclusion

By understanding the essentials of travel in Mumbai, you can enhance your experience and make the most of your time in this dynamic city. Each neighborhood and attraction has its own rhythm and unique appeal, offering a balance between old-world charm and modern excitement. With these practical insights and an open mind, you're set to explore Mumbai with confidence, respect, and curiosity, immersing yourself in the city's spirit and all that it has to offer.

Visa Requirements

Navigating the visa process is a key step in planning a smooth and enjoyable trip to Mumbai. The Indian government offers various visa options depending on the purpose, duration, and nature of your visit, from short tourism stays to longer business or study endeavors. Here, we'll outline the most commonly used visas for travelers visiting Mumbai, including details on eligibility, application procedures, and essential tips to ensure your entry to India is as seamless as possible.

Types of Tourist Visas

For most visitors traveling to Mumbai for leisure, exploration, or short-term visits, the Indian Tourist Visa and the e-Visa are the primary options:

- Tourist Visa: Typically issued for a period of six months to five years, depending on the applicant's nationality and individual requirements. With this visa, you can stay in India for up to 90 days per visit, though some countries may have shorter or longer maximum stays. Tourist visas can be obtained from Indian embassies or consulates in your home country. This option is ideal if you plan to travel frequently to India within the visa's validity period.

- e-Visa: Conveniently, India offers an e-Visa service for nationals of over 160 countries, allowing you to apply online before departure. The e-Visa is generally issued for short-term stays (30 to 90 days), covering categories such as tourism, business, and medical visits. It's valid for entry at select airports, including Mumbai's Chhatrapati Shivaji Maharaj International Airport, and simplifies the process by allowing you to complete the application and payment online, avoiding embassy visits.

Applying for the Indian e-Visa: A Step-by-Step Guide

If you're eligible for an e-Visa, this option is highly recommended for its convenience and time-saving benefits. Here's how to go through the application:

1. Start the Application Process Early: It's best to apply at least four days before your planned travel date, though applications can be submitted as early as 120 days before arrival. Processing times vary, but approvals typically take around three business days.

2. Prepare Required Documents:

    - Passport: You'll need a valid passport with at least six months of remaining validity from your date of arrival, and at least two blank pages.

    - Photograph: A recent passport-sized photograph (digital format) is required. Follow the specifications on the application site to avoid delays.

    - Other Documents: In some cases, proof of onward travel or accommodation details may be requested, though these are usually rare.

3. Complete the Application Form: Visit the official Indian government e-Visa website (https://indianvisaonline.gov.in) and fill in the required details, including your personal information, passport details, and travel itinerary.

4. Pay the Visa Fee: Fees vary depending on your nationality and visa type. Payments are made online, and a receipt will be provided. Be sure to retain it for reference.

5. Receive the e-Visa Approval: Once approved, your e-Visa will be sent to your registered email. Print out a copy, as you'll need to present it upon arrival at immigration.

Visa on Arrival (Limited to Japanese and South Korean Citizens)

India also offers a Visa on Arrival option specifically for citizens of Japan and South Korea. This is valid for stays of up to 60 days and allows two entries into the country within the validity period. While the Visa on Arrival can be convenient, travelers are advised to bring all necessary documentation to streamline the process at immigration.

Additional Visa Types

- Business Visa: For travelers visiting Mumbai for business meetings, conferences, or commercial activities, a business visa is available. This typically allows multiple entries over a period of up to one year or longer, depending on your nationality and the purpose of your visit.

- Employment Visa: If you're planning to work in Mumbai, an employment visa is essential. This requires a formal job offer from an Indian company, and the application process involves additional documents, such as proof of employment, qualifications, and letters from the employer.

- Student Visa: Students enrolled in long-term courses at Indian educational institutions can apply for a student visa, valid for the duration of their studies. Additional documentation, including admission letters and proof of financial resources, is required.

- Medical Visa: Travelers seeking medical treatment in Mumbai can apply for a medical visa. This visa allows for multiple entries over a shorter period and is ideal for those seeking specialized care in India's healthcare facilities.

Key Points to Remember

1. Check the Latest Requirements: Visa rules can change, so it's essential to check the latest requirements and guidelines through official channels, such as the Indian embassy or consulate in your country or the Indian government's official visa website.

2. Entry and Exit Points: India has specific entry and exit points designated for each visa type. For e-Visa holders, entry is permitted only at certain airports and seaports. Ensure you plan your journey accordingly.

3. Overstaying Penalties: Overstaying your visa in India is a serious offense that can result in fines, detention, or deportation. Make sure you're aware of the visa's expiration date and plan accordingly to avoid complications.

4. Health and Travel Insurance: While not a visa requirement, it's advisable to carry comprehensive travel insurance, especially if you're visiting India for extended periods. Coverage for health emergencies, theft, and cancellations can provide peace of mind during your travels.

Arriving in Mumbai: Immigration and Customs

Upon arrival at Mumbai's Chhatrapati Shivaji Maharaj International Airport, proceed to the immigration counters where you'll need to present your passport, visa, and e-Visa printout (if applicable). The immigration officers may ask basic questions regarding your stay, so having details of your accommodation and itinerary can be helpful. Following immigration, you'll move to customs, where you must declare any restricted items, such as high-value electronics or certain foods. Mumbai's customs and immigration procedures are generally straightforward, but patience is helpful as lines may be long.

Conclusion

Ensuring you have the right visa for your journey to Mumbai can set the stage for a hassle-free experience, giving you more time to immerse yourself in the city's culture, history, and attractions. From exploring the energetic markets of Colaba to unwinding by Marine Drive, Mumbai's allure is boundless. With your visa and travel plans in place, you'll be ready to dive into the many layers of India's iconic City of Dreams.

Chapter 1

Getting to Know Mumbai

Mumbai, often known as the City of Dreams, is a vibrant blend of history, diverse cultures, and relentless energy. Before setting out to explore its bustling streets and serene waterfronts, let's dive into Mumbai's fascinating evolution, its people and traditions, and the essentials you'll need to navigate this dynamic city.

A Brief History of Mumbai

Mumbai's transformation from a series of seven small islands into India's financial powerhouse is a story of resilience and vision. Originally inhabited by the Koli fishing communities and known as Heptanesia to early Greek geographers, Mumbai's journey took shape through waves of foreign influence and colonial expansion.

The Portuguese were the first Europeans to occupy Mumbai in the 16th century, naming it "Bom Bahia" (Good Bay). They eventually ceded it to the British Empire as part of a dowry when Catherine of Braganza married Charles II in 1661. Under British rule, these scattered islands were merged through a series of ambitious reclamation projects, turning them into the unified landmass we recognize today. This period also marked the rise of Bombay (now Mumbai) as a critical port, attracting traders, merchants, and fortune-seekers from across the globe.

By the mid-19th century, Bombay was a bustling hub of commerce and industry, spurred by its cotton trade and strategic location. The city's infrastructure expanded rapidly with the construction of railways, ports, and iconic colonial structures like the Gateway of India. Post-independence, Bombay became Mumbai, its original Marathi name, and embarked on a new era as a national center for commerce, cinema, and innovation. Today, Mumbai stands as India's largest city and a thriving testament to a cosmopolitan identity forged over centuries.

Culture and People: Embracing Mumbai's Melting Pot of Traditions

One of Mumbai's defining characteristics is its diverse and inclusive culture. People from all across India and beyond have made Mumbai their home, bringing with them a mosaic of languages, religions, and customs. This cultural melting pot fosters a unique social harmony and sense of shared purpose among Mumbaikars, as residents are called.

Mumbai is known for its spirit of resilience and community. Despite the pressures of urban life, people here are quick to lend a helping hand, a quality highlighted in times of hardship, such as the annual monsoon floods. The city's diversity is visible everywhere—from the grand temples, mosques, and churches that dot the skyline to the vibrant festivals celebrated year-round. Ganesh Chaturthi, for instance, is one of the most eagerly awaited festivals, bringing the city to life with colorful processions and immense devotion.

The arts play a significant role in Mumbai's culture. Home to Bollywood, the world's largest film industry, Mumbai is a hub for actors, musicians, and artists. The city also boasts an active theater scene, with performances in English, Hindi, and Marathi, catering to varied tastes. From street markets and galleries to upscale restaurants and festivals, Mumbai offers a rich cultural experience that balances traditional values with modern aspirations.

Quick Facts: Language, Currency, and Local Customs

Language: Marathi is Mumbai's official language, but Hindi and English are widely spoken, especially in business and tourism. The city's multilingual fabric also includes Gujarati, Tamil, and Urdu, reflecting the diverse communities residing here.

Currency: The Indian Rupee (INR) is the official currency. ATMs are plentiful, and most hotels, restaurants, and shops accept credit and debit cards. However, it's helpful to carry small amounts of cash for local markets, street food, and public transport.

Local Customs: Mumbai embraces an informal yet respectful culture. When visiting temples or places of worship, remember to dress modestly and remove your shoes before entering. Greetings vary depending on the setting; a simple "Namaste" or "Hello" is generally well-received. Tipping is customary in Mumbai, especially in restaurants, where a 10-15% tip is standard if service charges are not included.

Mumbai is a fast-paced city, and locals are accustomed to a bustling rhythm. Punctuality may not always be adhered to, but courtesy and respect are held in high regard. Bargaining is common in street markets and smaller shops, though it's done politely and is considered part of the shopping experience.

Navigating the City: Transportation Options and Tips for Getting Around

Mumbai's expansive transport system offers several ways to explore the city, each with its unique experience. From local trains to ride-sharing apps, here's a breakdown of the options and tips to navigate Mumbai efficiently:

- Local Trains: Known as the city's lifeline, Mumbai's suburban railway network is one of the busiest in the world, connecting the suburbs to the city center. Trains are categorized into Western, Central, and Harbour lines, with each line serving different areas. While affordable and efficient, rush hours can be extremely crowded, so it's best to travel outside peak times if possible. Women's-only compartments and first-class tickets offer a slightly more comfortable journey.

- BEST Buses: Mumbai's BEST (Brihanmumbai Electric Supply and Transport) buses are a great way to explore the city at a leisurely pace. They cover extensive routes, including areas where trains may not reach. The double-decker buses, a nostalgic Mumbai icon, are particularly scenic for sightseeing. While fares are inexpensive, traffic congestion can make travel times unpredictable.

- Auto Rickshaws and Taxis: Auto rickshaws (autos) and black-and-yellow taxis are convenient for short distances. Auto rickshaws primarily operate in the suburbs and do not enter the city center, while taxis are available citywide. Metered fares are standard, though negotiating or confirming the fare before starting the trip is wise, especially at night. Ride-sharing apps like Uber and Ola offer added convenience and safety.

- Mumbai Metro: The Mumbai Metro is a newer addition to the city's transport landscape, expanding to connect different parts of the city in a comfortable and air-conditioned environment. While the metro network is still growing, it offers an efficient alternative to crowded trains and congested roads in the areas it serves.

- Ferries and Water Taxis: Mumbai's coastal geography makes ferries a viable option for exploring nearby islands and coastal points. Ferries operate from Gateway of India to popular destinations like Elephanta Island and Alibaug. Water taxis are also an emerging service, though currently limited in availability.

Getting Around Tips:

1. Plan for Traffic: Mumbai's streets are often congested, especially during peak hours (9–11 a.m. and 6–9 p.m.). For longer distances, consider the train or metro if it covers your destination, or plan for additional travel time if using buses or taxis.

2. Use Ride-Share Apps for Safety and Convenience: Apps like Uber and Ola provide a safe and reliable option, especially at night or in unfamiliar areas. Fares are transparent, and the GPS-based service adds a layer of security for solo travelers.

3. Stay Hydrated and Prepare for Heat: Mumbai's tropical climate can be intense, particularly during summer. Carry a water bottle, stay hydrated, and wear light clothing when traveling around the city.

4. Purchase a Local SIM Card: Access to mobile data can be invaluable for navigating the city, checking routes, or booking rides. Many kiosks at the airport and around the city offer affordable SIM cards with data plans.

5. Respect Local Etiquette: Mumbai's fast-paced lifestyle may seem overwhelming at first, but understanding local etiquette can make a difference. For instance, always form queues at ticket counters and don't be alarmed if you encounter crowds, especially in public transit.

Getting to know Mumbai before setting out to explore its sights can enrich your experience and provide practical insights into the city's heartbeat. Whether you're navigating a crowded train or bargaining in the vibrant street markets, this chapter will equip you with the knowledge and confidence to start your journey through one of India's most captivating cities.

Chapter 2

Iconic Landmarks of Mumbai

Mumbai is a city where the old and new exist side by side, and its landmarks reflect a deep blend of history, spirituality, and scenic beauty. From the grandiose colonial architecture of the British era to spiritual sanctuaries that draw thousands of pilgrims, Mumbai's iconic landmarks are a testament to its rich heritage and vibrant energy. In this chapter, we'll explore some of the city's most celebrated attractions, offering historical context, travel tips, and insights to help you experience each site fully.

The Gateway of India: Historical Significance and Visitor Tips

The Gateway of India is perhaps Mumbai's most recognized symbol. Built in 1924, this magnificent arch was constructed to commemorate the arrival of King George V and Queen Mary to India in 1911. Designed by George Wittet, the structure features Indo-Saracenic architecture, a style that blends Indian, Islamic, and European influences. The Gateway's colossal basalt structure overlooks the Arabian Sea, making it a striking welcome to Mumbai's shores.

Originally intended as a ceremonial entrance for British officials, the Gateway has since witnessed pivotal moments in Indian history, including the departure of British troops in 1948, symbolizing the end of colonial rule. Today, it's a popular meeting point for locals and tourists alike, with vibrant street vendors and boat trips to nearby Elephanta Island.

Visitor Tips:

- Best Time to Visit: Early morning or late evening when the crowds are thinner, and the lighting over the sea is beautiful.

- Photography: Capture the Gateway's intricate details up close or take panoramic shots that include the adjacent Taj Mahal Palace Hotel.

- Nearby Activities: Consider taking a ferry from here to Elephanta Island, an excellent day trip to ancient rock-cut caves that are a UNESCO World Heritage Site.

Chhatrapati Shivaji Maharaj Terminus: A UNESCO Heritage Marvel

Formerly known as Victoria Terminus, the Chhatrapati Shivaji Maharaj Terminus (CSMT) is a stunning example of Victorian Gothic architecture infused with Indian design elements. This grand railway station, completed in 1887 by British architect Frederick William Stevens, serves as the headquarters for the Central Railways. In 2004, it earned a spot on the UNESCO World Heritage list, celebrated for its intricate detailing, pointed arches, domes, and spires.

Beyond its architectural splendor, CSMT is one of Mumbai's busiest transport hubs, where millions of commuters pass through daily. It's a microcosm of Mumbai's energy, with its bustling platforms and constant flow of people, giving a glimpse into the city's fast-paced life.

Visitor Tips:

- Admire the Architecture: Take time to explore the station's exteriors and interiors to appreciate the stone carvings, stained glass windows, and Gothic arches. Look out for gargoyles and figures of animals, blending traditional Indian and Western architectural styles.

- Photography Permits: The station's heritage wing sometimes requires special permits for professional photography; inquire ahead of your visit.

- Nearby Attractions: CSMT is centrally located near other colonial-era buildings like Mumbai Municipal Corporation and Flora Fountain, ideal for a heritage walk around South Mumbai.

Marine Drive and the Queen's Necklace: Coastal Beauty and Evening Walks

Marine Drive, affectionately known as the Queen's Necklace for its sweeping, crescent shape illuminated by street lights at night, is an iconic coastal boulevard stretching along the Arabian Sea. Built in the 1920s, Marine Drive embodies the art deco style that defined much of South Mumbai's early architecture. This promenade is an essential part of daily life for Mumbaikars, offering a peaceful respite from the city's rush and a fantastic spot to watch the sunset.

The 3.6-kilometer stretch of Marine Drive is especially popular in the evenings, with people from all walks of life gathering to enjoy the refreshing sea breeze. The view of the sea and the sight of the city's skyline transitioning from day to night make it a memorable experience.

Visitor Tips:

- Timing: Visit at sunset or after dark when the entire promenade is lit up, creating the illusion of a dazzling necklace.

- Walking the Boulevard: Stroll along Marine Drive from Nariman Point to Chowpatty Beach, where you can enjoy local snacks like bhel puri and pav bhaji at the open-air stalls.

- Stay Safe: While generally safe, Marine Drive can get crowded. Keep an eye on your belongings and enjoy the scenery.

Haji Ali Dargah: Pilgrimage Site and Architectural Wonder

The Haji Ali Dargah is a revered mosque and shrine situated on a small islet off the coast of Worli, dedicated to Saint Haji Ali, a wealthy merchant who gave up his material possessions to embark on a spiritual journey. Built in the 15th century, the shrine features Indo-Islamic architecture and is known for its ethereal setting, accessible only during low tide by a narrow causeway.

Haji Ali's unique location and spiritual ambiance make it a major pilgrimage site for people of all faiths, symbolizing Mumbai's tradition of religious tolerance. The shrine is particularly striking at sunset, silhouetted against the horizon with waves lapping at its foundation.

Visitor Tips:

- Access: Check the tide schedule before visiting, as the path is submerged during high tide.

- Respectful Dress Code: Wear modest clothing, as this is a sacred site. Women should cover their heads before entering the shrine.

- Photography: Capture shots of the shrine from the causeway or from a distance to include its stunning sea surroundings.

Siddhivinayak Temple: Spiritual Significance and Local Devotion

Located in Prabhadevi, the Siddhivinayak Temple is one of Mumbai's most important and frequently visited temples, dedicated to Lord Ganesha, the elephant-headed deity symbolizing wisdom and prosperity. Built in 1801, the temple has grown in popularity and is especially crowded on Tuesdays, a day considered auspicious for Ganesha worship.

Siddhivinayak Temple is a harmonious blend of spirituality and modern architecture, with a central dome adorned with gold and intricately carved wooden doors that depict various forms of Ganesha. Devotees often offer sweets and flowers, seeking blessings for success and well-being. The temple is also known for attracting Bollywood stars and politicians, adding to its fame.

Visitor Tips:

- Timing: To avoid the large crowds, visit on weekdays or early in the morning.

- Offerings: Modest offerings such as flowers, sweets, or coconut are appreciated, and you can find vendors selling these near the temple entrance.

- Security: As it is a popular religious site, there are security checks at the entrance. Avoid bringing large bags or valuables.

Mumbai's landmarks offer a window into the city's soul, from the colonial elegance of the Gateway of India and CSMT to the spiritual allure of Siddhivinayak and Haji Ali. Each site presents a facet of Mumbai's complex identity, revealing the city's historical depth, coastal charm, and unwavering devotion. These must-see destinations make up the foundation of any visit to Mumbai, inviting you to connect with the legacy and energy that define this extraordinary city.

Chapter 3

Exploring Mumbai's Neighborhoods

Mumbai's neighborhoods each have a distinct character, offering diverse experiences that capture the city's rich tapestry of cultures, lifestyles, and histories. From the colonial charm of Colaba to the artistic corners of Kala Ghoda and the bustling celebrity hub of Bandra, each area provides a unique window into Mumbai's multifaceted soul. This chapter takes you on a journey through some of Mumbai's most popular neighborhoods, providing insider tips and highlights to make the most of your visit.

Colaba: Shopping, Dining, and Famous Sights

Colaba is a vibrant neighborhood at the southern tip of Mumbai, known for its historical landmarks, bustling markets, and eclectic mix of cafes and restaurants. Colaba Causeway is the area's main artery, where vendors line the streets selling everything from jewelry and trinkets to antiques and designer knock-offs. This lively stretch is a haven for shoppers and those looking to soak up Mumbai's lively street culture.

Beyond shopping, Colaba boasts some of Mumbai's most iconic sites. The Gateway of India is a must-visit, as is the Taj Mahal Palace Hotel across the road, offering a striking juxtaposition of colonial architecture and Indian opulence. For dining, Colaba offers a range of options from fine dining to street food, making it a perfect spot to experience the best of Mumbai's culinary landscape.

Highlights:

- Leopold Café and Café Mondegar: Two legendary cafes where travelers, locals, and artists meet for hearty meals and conversation.

- Colaba Causeway: Ideal for picking up souvenirs and unique finds; be ready to haggle for the best price.

- Art Galleries: Colaba is home to several art galleries, including the National Gallery of Modern Art (NGMA), showcasing both modern Indian and international art.

Fort and Kala Ghoda: Art, Architecture, and Cafés

The Fort area and the neighboring Kala Ghoda district are synonymous with Mumbai's colonial architecture, art scene, and trendy cafes. Known for its heritage buildings, Fort houses impressive structures like the Chhatrapati Shivaji Maharaj Terminus, the Bombay High Court, and Flora Fountain. The Kala Ghoda district, meanwhile, has grown into Mumbai's art hub, filled with galleries, studios, and street art.

Each February, the Kala Ghoda Arts Festival takes over the streets, featuring an exciting mix of installations, performances, and workshops that draw artists and tourists from all over the world. If you're an art lover, don't miss Jehangir Art Gallery, where contemporary Indian artists often exhibit their work. In addition to art and architecture, the area is known for its stylish cafes, offering a laid-back atmosphere ideal for people-watching or taking a break from exploring.

Highlights:

- Architecture Walks: Join a guided tour to delve into the rich history and architectural significance of the buildings in Fort and Kala Ghoda.

- Cafés: Grab a coffee at Kala Ghoda Café or The Pantry—perfect spots to unwind while exploring the art district.

- Street Art: Wander around to see colorful murals and graffiti, showcasing the vibrant creativity that defines the area.

Bandra: The Celebrity Hub, Street Art, and Trendy Spots

Bandra is often called the "Queen of Suburbs" and is known for its bohemian vibe, celebrity residences, and trendy cafes. Here, Bollywood stars rub shoulders with street artists, and upscale restaurants coexist with local food joints. Mount Mary's Basilica offers a peaceful retreat, while Bandra Fort provides stunning views of the sea and the Bandra-Worli Sea Link. The bylanes of Bandra are adorned with street art, depicting everything from Bollywood legends to social messages, adding color and character to the neighborhood.

For celebrity spotters, Bandra is the place to be. The posh streets of Pali Hill and Bandra Bandstand are home to Bollywood stars like Shah Rukh Khan, whose bungalow "Mannat" is a pilgrimage site for fans. Bandra's food scene is just as diverse as its residents, offering everything from global cuisine to authentic local flavors, with countless cafes and bars adding to its lively nightlife.

Highlights:

- Bandra Street Art Tour: Explore vibrant murals and graffiti by Indian and international artists; take photos as you stroll through the colorful lanes.
- Celebrity Homes: Pass by the famous residences of Bollywood stars at Pali Hill and Bandstand.
- Nightlife: Bandra has a buzzing nightlife scene with popular spots like Olive Bar & Kitchen and Pali Village Café.

Juhu and Versova: Beaches, Bollywood, and Food Culture

Juhu is known for its iconic Juhu Beach, a sprawling stretch of sand that's especially popular at sunset. Here, locals and tourists alike gather to enjoy the cool sea breeze, sample street food from the stalls along the shore, and catch a glimpse of Bollywood stars who frequent the area. Versova Beach lies further north, quieter and less commercialized than Juhu, and is ideal for those seeking a peaceful seaside experience.

Juhu is also home to some of Mumbai's most luxurious properties and high-profile residents, including Bollywood celebrities. You'll find an array of eateries in this neighborhood, from high-end restaurants to beachside stalls offering Mumbai's signature snacks like pani puri and pav bhaji. The area's cosmopolitan vibe and proximity to Bollywood studios make it a key location for film shoots and celebrity sightings.

Highlights:

- Juhu Beach: Enjoy local snacks like bhel puri and vada pav as you take in the lively beach atmosphere.

- Versova Beach Clean-Up: Known for its environmental efforts, the beach frequently hosts community clean-ups; you may even spot actor volunteers supporting the cause.

- Luxury Dining: Experience upscale dining at popular restaurants such as Estella and JW Marriott's Lotus Café.

Dharavi: Understanding Asia's Largest Slum with Ethical Tours

Dharavi is often referred to as Asia's largest slum, yet it's much more than the stereotypes suggest. Dharavi is a vibrant community with thriving industries, including pottery, leather, textiles, and recycling. Ethical tours offer visitors the chance to understand the daily lives of Dharavi's residents, showcasing the resilience, talent, and entrepreneurial spirit that define this area.

Walking tours led by local guides allow visitors to learn about Dharavi's economy, its unique social structure, and its role in Mumbai's recycling efforts. These tours emphasize respect and ethical travel, aiming to challenge misconceptions and provide a meaningful perspective on the community's contributions to Mumbai's economy.

Highlights:

- Ethical Walking Tours: Opt for tours led by responsible operators such as Reality Tours & Travel, who donate a portion of their profits back to the community.

- Pottery and Leather Workshops: See skilled artisans in action, and if time allows, participate in a workshop or purchase handmade goods directly from the makers.

- Recycling Hub: Dharavi's recycling industry is impressive; learn how materials are sorted, processed, and upcycled by small-scale factories that support the local economy.

Each of these neighborhoods offers a unique glimpse into the city of Mumbai, showcasing different aspects of its dynamic culture, lifestyle, and heritage. From the colonial elegance of Colaba to the creative spirit of Bandra and the entrepreneurial drive of Dharavi, Mumbai's neighborhoods are as diverse as its people. Whether you're seeking art, history, relaxation, or adventure, exploring these areas will give you a deeper appreciation for what makes Mumbai one of the world's most intriguing cities.

Chapter 4

Mumbai's Cultural Scene

Mumbai, the cultural heart of India, is a city that pulses with artistic expression, spiritual celebrations, and a love for cinema. This chapter dives into the elements that make Mumbai's cultural landscape vibrant and diverse, from the glitz and glamour of Bollywood to the rich tapestry of festivals and traditional performances. Mumbai's thriving art scene and deep-rooted love for music and dance reflect the city's unique blend of tradition and modernity.

Bollywood and Beyond

Bollywood, the world's largest film industry in terms of production, is synonymous with Mumbai. For anyone intrigued by Indian cinema, Mumbai offers an exciting behind-the-scenes look at this glittering world. Film City, located in Goregaon, is a popular site for tours that showcase movie sets, production areas, and sometimes even live shoots, allowing you to experience the thrill of Bollywood firsthand. Private tours of studios like Yash Raj Studios provide a curated insight into filmmaking and highlight the immense industry machinery behind India's famous cinema.

Mumbai is also dotted with homes of Bollywood stars, particularly in areas like Juhu and Bandra. While these neighborhoods are mostly residential, star sightings are common in the cafes and streets nearby, particularly around Bandra Bandstand. For a truly immersive Bollywood experience, don't miss watching a movie in one of Mumbai's historic cinemas, such as Maratha Mandir or Regal Cinema. The audience's enthusiasm and the grandeur of the theaters make it a cultural experience in itself.

Highlights:

- Film City Tours: Explore sets, backdrops, and production areas in the heart of Bollywood's studio complex.
- Celebrity Homes: Juhu and Bandra are prime areas for catching a glimpse of Bollywood stars; guided celebrity tours are available for those keen on star-spotting.
- Historic Cinemas: Watching a Bollywood film in Maratha Mandir or Eros Cinema is a lively experience, complete with cheering crowds and colorful dance scenes.

Art and Museums

Mumbai's art scene is as eclectic as its people, offering everything from contemporary installations to heritage collections. Jehangir Art Gallery, situated in the cultural district of Kala Ghoda, is a prestigious space that showcases the works of Indian artists, both emerging and established. Exhibitions change frequently, ensuring there's always something new to discover, from modern art to traditional Indian works.

The National Gallery of Modern Art (NGMA) is another gem, featuring a curated collection of 19th and 20th-century art, including paintings, sculptures, and photographs. The museum hosts exhibitions that often highlight India's art movements, providing valuable insights into the evolution of Indian aesthetics.

For those interested in the city's history, the Dr. Bhau Daji Lad Museum is a must-visit. This museum offers a rich narrative of Mumbai's development, including its colonial past and the cultural influences that have shaped the city. Known for its beautiful Victorian architecture and detailed displays, the museum also has fascinating artifacts, such as maps, photographs, and decorative arts from the 19th century, painting a vivid picture of Mumbai's historical and artistic heritage.

Highlights:

- Jehangir Art Gallery: Rotating exhibitions make this a go-to spot for anyone interested in contemporary Indian art.

- NGMA: Delve into the history of Indian art movements through the extensive collections and themed exhibitions.

- Dr. Bhau Daji Lad Museum: This Victorian gem offers a historical perspective on Mumbai through intricate displays and artifacts.

Traditional Festivals: Ganesh Chaturthi, Diwali, and Other Celebrations

Mumbai's cultural vibrancy truly shines during its traditional festivals, celebrated with immense passion and grandeur. Ganesh Chaturthi, honoring the elephant-headed god Ganesha, is perhaps the city's most iconic festival. During this time, Mumbai is adorned with temporary temples and elaborate idols of Ganesha, and the streets are filled with music, dance, and processions. The final day of the festival sees thousands of devotees gather on Mumbai's beaches to immerse the idols, creating a spectacular and emotional scene.

Diwali, the festival of lights, illuminates every corner of Mumbai, as homes and businesses are decorated with lamps, rangolis, and fireworks. It's a joyous occasion marked by family gatherings, sweets, and traditional performances, providing a warm glimpse into Indian hospitality and customs. Other notable festivals include Navratri, when Mumbai is abuzz with nine nights of traditional dance and music, and Eid, celebrated with grand feasts and community events, particularly around Mohammed Ali Road.

Highlights:

- Ganesh Chaturthi Processions: Visiting a Ganesha pandal or watching the grand visarjan (immersion) ceremony at Chowpatty Beach is unforgettable.
- Diwali Celebrations: Experience the city's festive lights, firecrackers, and the contagious joy that fills the air.
- Navratri: Join in on the Garba and Dandiya dances, which take place in large, colorful venues across the city.

Music and Dance: Classical, Contemporary, and Street Performances

Mumbai's music and dance scene reflects India's artistic diversity, blending traditional styles with contemporary influences. Classical music has a strong presence here, with events such as the Sawai Gandharva Bhimsen Mahotsav and the Banganga Music Festival attracting renowned classical musicians. These concerts, often held in historic venues, offer an opportunity to witness India's classical traditions in an intimate and reverent setting.

Contemporary music, particularly Bollywood, pop, and electronic, is equally popular. Venues like Blue Frog and Antisocial are celebrated for their live performances, ranging from indie artists to international DJs, making them hot spots for Mumbai's music lovers. Street performances are also common, especially in neighborhoods like Kala Ghoda, where you can see everything from folk dancers to freestyle rappers showcasing their talents.

Dance, too, plays an essential role in Mumbai's cultural identity. From classical Indian dance forms like Kathak and Bharatanatyam to street hip-hop and Bollywood-style dances, Mumbai's dance culture is as dynamic as its people. Prithvi Theatre in Juhu is known for its cultural events and performances, while large festivals like Kala Ghoda Arts Festival feature live dance performances across various genres, providing visitors with an immersive experience.

Highlights:

- Classical Music Festivals: Attend performances by India's best classical musicians at events like the Banganga Festival for a serene musical experience.
- Contemporary Music Venues: Blue Frog and other venues offer a taste of Mumbai's vibrant nightlife with live music from Indian and international artists.
- Dance Events: Watch performances of classical Indian dance or Bollywood-style dance-offs at Prithvi Theatre and street festivals.

Mumbai's cultural scene offers a unique blend of the traditional and the modern, creating an environment where art, music, cinema, and festivals come together to form a rich tapestry. This chapter provides a comprehensive guide to exploring these cultural gems, allowing visitors to connect deeply with the city's artistic and celebratory spirit. Whether you're catching a Bollywood film, watching a classical music recital, or witnessing a colorful festival, Mumbai's cultural experiences are sure to leave you captivated.

Chapter 5

Culinary Journey Through Mumbai

Mumbai's culinary landscape is a vibrant and delicious fusion of flavors, reflecting the city's multicultural heritage and love for bold, spice-rich foods. From the irresistible aromas of its iconic street food to the refined elegance of its fine dining establishments, Mumbai is a paradise for food lovers. This chapter takes you on a deep dive into Mumbai's culinary scene, covering everything from must-try dishes to immersive food tours that reveal the city's gastronomic soul.

An Introduction to Mumbai Cuisine

Mumbai's cuisine is as dynamic as the city itself. A melting pot of cultures, it brings together flavors from various Indian regions, blending them with influences from Persian, Arabic, and even Portuguese cuisine. At its heart is street food, which defines the city's culinary identity and provides an authentic taste of its fast-paced, diverse character. From fiery snacks to refreshing chaats, Mumbai's street food scene is legendary, offering dishes that cater to every palate and pocket.

But there's more to Mumbai than its street fare. In recent years, the city has witnessed a boom in fusion cuisine, where traditional recipes meet global flavors. This has given rise to innovative dishes that reinterpret classics with modern twists, such as tandoori pizzas, pav bhaji fondue, and spicy pani puri shots. Signature dishes—like the humble yet addictive vada pav, creamy butter chicken, and fragrant seafood curries—remain staples, revered by locals and travelers alike. Exploring Mumbai's culinary landscape means embracing both the old and the new, the rustic and the refined.

Must-Try Dishes: Vada Pav, Pav Bhaji, Bhel Puri, Pani Puri, and More

No culinary journey through Mumbai would be complete without sampling the city's signature street foods. Here are a few must-try dishes that embody the spirit and flavor of Mumbai:

- Vada Pav: Known as Mumbai's "poor man's burger," vada pav is a spicy, deep-fried potato dumpling served in a soft bun with a variety of chutneys and green chili. It's inexpensive, satisfying, and deeply ingrained in Mumbai's street food culture.

- Pav Bhaji: A hearty dish of mashed vegetables cooked with butter and spices, pav bhaji is served with buttered bread rolls (pav) and topped with fresh onions and lemon. This popular meal began as a late-night snack for laborers but is now enjoyed across the city.

- Bhel Puri: A refreshing and crunchy mix of puffed rice, sev (fried chickpea noodles), vegetables, and tangy tamarind chutney, bhel puri offers a balanced blend of sweet, spicy, and sour flavors. It's a perfect snack for those looking for a lighter option.

- Pani Puri: Known as golgappa in northern India, pani puri is a fun and interactive snack of hollow, crispy puris filled with spicy, tangy water, mashed potatoes, and chickpeas. It's served quickly by street vendors, and eating it is a communal experience.

- Keema Pav: This dish consists of spiced minced meat (usually mutton) served with soft bread rolls. Keema pav is often enjoyed as a breakfast item but can be found in cafes and eateries throughout the day.

- Bombay Sandwich: Made with layers of fresh vegetables, green chutney, and butter, the Bombay sandwich is a quick and satisfying snack. Often toasted to a crispy perfection, it's a crowd favorite at roadside stalls.

Tip: While sampling these treats, remember to ask for mild spice if you're not accustomed to Mumbai's heat-packed flavors!

Street Food Hotspots: Khau Gallis, Chowpatty Beach, and Local Markets

Mumbai's street food is best experienced in its vibrant "khau gallis" (food streets), bustling markets, and iconic beach fronts where vendors serve piping-hot delicacies to eager customers. Some of the best spots to savor Mumbai's street food are:

- Khau Gallis: Mumbai is famous for its khau gallis, or food lanes, where rows of vendors serve fresh, affordable, and flavorful street food. The CST Khau Galli and Tardeo Khau Galli are especially popular, offering everything from dosa to pav bhaji and jalebi.

- Chowpatty Beach: Located in Girgaum, Chowpatty Beach is not only a scenic spot but also a beloved destination for street food. Here, you can find vendors serving bhel puri, pav bhaji, and kulfi (Indian ice cream) against the backdrop of the Arabian Sea. The atmosphere is relaxed, especially at sunset, making it an ideal spot for food lovers to gather.

- Juhu Beach: Juhu Beach is another popular spot to enjoy Mumbai's street food. Like Chowpatty, it's famous for its bhel puri, pani puri, and ragda pattice. The energy is vibrant, and you'll often see families, friends, and couples sampling snacks while taking in the sea breeze.

- Crawford Market: While mainly known for groceries and textiles, Crawford Market also has a range of food stalls serving delicious quick bites. Don't miss the fresh juices and snacks here; they're a refreshing way to fuel up after shopping.

Fine Dining and Iconic Restaurants

Beyond street food, Mumbai's fine dining scene presents an array of flavors and textures, with restaurants offering everything from authentic Indian to world cuisine. For those looking to experience the best of Mumbai's culinary prowess, here are a few notable spots:

- Leopold Café: An institution in Colaba, Leopold Café is known for its rich history, laid-back atmosphere, and extensive menu that caters to both locals and tourists. Try the prawn biryani or butter chicken, paired with a cold Kingfisher beer.

- Britannia & Co.: A beloved Parsi restaurant located in Ballard Estate, Britannia is known for its berry pulao, mutton dhansak, and caramel custard. The restaurant's old-world charm and authentic Parsi dishes are an experience in themselves.

- Trishna: Located in Fort, Trishna is famous for its seafood, especially its butter garlic crab and prawn koliwada. The restaurant is known for its fresh ingredients and spicy flavors, making it a hit among locals and visitors alike.

- The Table: For a more modern dining experience, The Table in Colaba is a great choice. With a farm-to-table philosophy, it offers inventive dishes that blend global flavors with local ingredients.

- Masala Library: For those who want a taste of Indian cuisine with a contemporary twist, Masala Library offers molecular gastronomy and reimagined Indian classics. Dishes like the deconstructed samosa and jalebi caviar make for an unforgettable culinary experience.

Food Tours and Cooking Classes

For those who want a deeper dive into Mumbai's food culture, food tours and cooking classes offer an engaging and hands-on experience. These tours allow you to not only taste a variety of local dishes but also gain insights into the culinary techniques and ingredients that make Mumbai's food unique.

- Street Food Tours: Various operators in Mumbai offer guided street food tours, which take you through the best khau gallis and local markets. These tours are led by knowledgeable guides who can provide cultural context to the dishes and suggest must-try items, making it a great way to discover hidden gems and eat like a local.

- Cooking Classes: For an interactive experience, consider joining a cooking class. Many classes are hosted in local homes, allowing you to learn traditional recipes in an intimate setting. You'll get hands-on experience making dishes like paneer tikka, biryani, and chapati, with insights into spice selection and preparation techniques.

- Market Tours with Cooking Lessons: Some cooking classes also offer market tours, where you can explore local spice shops and vegetable markets before returning to cook a meal. These tours provide an excellent way to understand Mumbai's food supply chain, from fresh produce to the final dish.

Whether you're exploring Mumbai's bustling food streets or indulging in a fine dining experience, the city's culinary scene is an adventure in every bite. This chapter provides a roadmap for savoring Mumbai's flavors, helping you connect with the city through its most beloved foods and cherished dining spots.

Chapter 6

Shopping and Markets

Mumbai is a vibrant shopping destination where traditional markets and modern malls coexist, catering to every taste and budget. From colorful street stalls to upscale boutiques, Mumbai's shopping scene reflects the city's diverse culture and lively spirit. In this chapter, we'll explore the best places to shop, uncover unique finds, and share essential tips for navigating Mumbai's markets like a local.

Street Markets: Colaba Causeway, Fashion Street, and Crawford Market

Mumbai's street markets are bustling hubs where you can find everything from budget fashion to unique souvenirs, fresh produce, and handmade crafts. Here's a look at some of the city's most popular street shopping destinations.

- Colaba Causeway: Often called the "Queen of Street Markets," Colaba Causeway is a favorite spot for locals and tourists alike. Located near the Gateway of India, this market offers a little bit of everything—bohemian jewelry, handcrafted souvenirs, leather bags, shoes, and eclectic home decor. Colaba Causeway is also known for its unique mix of high-end boutiques and street vendors, making it an ideal spot for all budgets. Don't miss the chance to bargain; sellers expect it and are usually open to negotiating prices.

- Fashion Street: For budget-friendly fashion, Fashion Street on MG Road in South Mumbai is a must-visit. This market is packed with over 300 stalls selling trendy clothing, shoes, and accessories at low prices. Popular with students and young shoppers, Fashion Street is ideal for those who enjoy hunting for bargains. Keep in mind that sizes may be limited, and while the

- Crawford Market: One of Mumbai's oldest markets, Crawford Market is a bustling center for fresh produce, spices, and dry fruits, along with a range of imported goods. The market's colonial architecture adds to its charm, and inside, you'll find everything from exotic fruits to fragrant spices that you can take home as souvenirs. Crawford Market is particularly busy during holidays like Diwali, when vendors offer seasonal items such as decorations and sweets. For those interested in food photography, Crawford Market offers a fantastic visual experience with its vibrant colors and local hustle.

Local Art and Crafts: Souvenirs and Handicrafts to Take Home

Mumbai's rich cultural heritage is reflected in its handicrafts, textiles, and artisanal goods. From traditional block prints to handcrafted jewelry, the city offers unique items that make wonderful souvenirs or gifts.

- Handicrafts: Mumbai is known for a wide variety of traditional crafts, including Warli paintings, an art form by the Warli tribe of Maharashtra, which depict scenes of rural life using simple geometric shapes. You can find these at specialized stores like Chhatrapati Shivaji Maharaj Vastu Sangrahalaya's museum shop or at government emporiums.

- Jewelry and Trinkets: Head to the narrow lanes of Zaveri Bazaar if you're interested in authentic Indian jewelry, including intricate gold and silver pieces. This market has been a jewelry hub for centuries and offers everything from wedding jewelry to small, handcrafted trinkets. Street stalls near Colaba Causeway also offer affordable jewelry made of brass, silver, and even semi-precious stones.

- Block-Printed Textiles: India is famous for its vibrant textiles, and block-printing is an age-old technique that creates beautiful patterns on fabrics.

Stores like Fabindia and Khadi Bhandar in Mumbai specialize in block-printed clothing, scarves, and home decor items. These products make great gifts, adding a touch of India to your home or wardrobe.

- Leather Goods: Mumbai has several stores and markets offering quality leather goods. Dharavi, Asia's largest slum, is also known for its skilled leather artisans. Many local businesses now provide guided tours of Dharavi's leather workshops, where you can buy handmade leather bags, wallets, and jackets. This is an opportunity to purchase high-quality goods while supporting local artisans.

High-End Malls and Boutiques

For a more polished shopping experience, Mumbai's high-end malls and boutiques offer luxury brands and curated selections from Indian designers. These spaces blend international sophistication with local creativity, providing a contrast to the city's bustling street markets.

- High Street Phoenix and Palladium: Located in Lower Parel, High Street Phoenix and Palladium are among Mumbai's most upscale shopping destinations. Here, you'll find luxury brands like Gucci, Louis Vuitton, and Jimmy Choo, alongside Indian designer stores such as Anita Dongre and Tarun Tahiliani. The mall also features fine dining options and an art gallery, making it a complete luxury experience.

- Colaba Boutiques: Colaba is not just about street shopping; it's also home to some of Mumbai's most charming boutiques. Stores like Bungalow 8 and Bombay Electric showcase unique collections of clothing, home decor, and accessories crafted by Indian artisans and designers. The pieces here often reflect India's modern aesthetic blended with traditional craftsmanship, perfect for those looking to add distinctive items to their wardrobe or home.

- Linking Road, Bandra: While Linking Road is famous for its street shopping, it also has a collection of high-end stores and trendy boutiques. Known as a fashion hub, Bandra offers an eclectic mix of brands, from Zara and H&M to independent designers and bohemian shops. Linking Road is ideal for both high-street shoppers and those interested in luxury retail, offering a variety of options within walking distance.

- Kala Ghoda: For art lovers, the Kala Ghoda neighborhood offers a selection of art galleries and design studios featuring contemporary art, antique furniture, and handcrafted jewelry. A visit to this area provides a more refined and unique shopping experience, with opportunities to purchase exclusive Indian art and sculptures.

Tips for Bargaining and Navigating Mumbai's Markets

Mumbai's markets can be overwhelming for newcomers, especially when it comes to bargaining. Here are some practical tips to help you navigate the city's markets with ease:

1. Bargain Confidently: Bargaining is expected in most of Mumbai's street markets. As a general rule, start by offering half the quoted price, then work your way to a middle ground. Remember to be polite but firm, and approach bargaining as part of the shopping experience rather than a confrontation.

2. Bring Cash: While some vendors may accept digital payments, cash is still preferred, especially in smaller street markets. Carry smaller denominations, as vendors often don't have change for large bills. ATMs are readily available, but it's wise to have cash on hand before arriving at markets.

3. Dress Comfortably: Mumbai's markets are often crowded, so wearing comfortable clothes and shoes is essential. Protect yourself from the sun with a hat and carry a bottle of water. For women, a small crossbody bag is recommended, as it leaves your hands free and keeps belongings secure.

4. Beware of Fake Goods: Some street vendors may offer counterfeit versions of popular brands. If you're looking for authentic branded items, it's best to

stick to established stores and boutiques. For other items, the quality can vary, so inspect your purchases carefully before buying.

5. Shop Early: Some markets are less crowded in the morning, which can make for a more relaxed shopping experience. Vendors are often more willing to negotiate during these hours, as the first sale of the day is considered lucky. Visiting early can help you secure better deals and shop with ease.

6. Stay Aware of Your Surroundings: Mumbai's markets are generally safe, but it's always wise to keep an eye on your belongings. Carry a crossbody bag with a zipper and avoid displaying large amounts of cash or valuables.

Mumbai's markets and shopping districts offer a blend of high-energy bargaining and luxurious finds, providing a shopping experience that's as dynamic as the city itself. Whether you're on the hunt for affordable souvenirs, designer clothing, or handcrafted decor, Mumbai's shopping scene is an adventure waiting to be explored.

Practical Tips

Exploring Mumbai's outdoor activities can be a fantastic way to experience the city's natural beauty and diverse landscapes. Here are some practical tips to help you make the most of your excursions:

1. Visiting Mumbai's Beaches

- Best Time to Visit: Early mornings and late afternoons are the best times to visit beaches in Mumbai, as midday can be quite hot, especially during the summer. The winter months (November to February) are ideal for beach outings, with pleasant temperatures and minimal humidity.

- Avoid Swimming in Some Areas: While some beaches like Aksa and Versova are beautiful, their waters are often unsafe for swimming due to strong currents and occasional pollution. Juhu Beach and Girgaum

Chowpatty are popular for walking and dining but not ideal for a swim. Always look out for local advice and follow any warning signs.

- **Safety and Cleanliness:** Beaches can get crowded, so keep an eye on your belongings, especially during weekends and festivals. Bringing a reusable bag for any waste can help keep the beaches clean, as waste bins can sometimes be scarce.

2. Exploring Sanjay Gandhi National Park

- **Permits and Entry Fees:** The park charges a nominal entry fee, and additional fees apply for guided tours and access to the Kanheri Caves. Permits for trekking and certain areas of the park may be required, so it's best to check in advance if you plan to explore deeply.

- **Dress Comfortably and Prepare for the Outdoors:** Wear comfortable, breathable clothing, and bring sturdy walking shoes, especially if you plan to trek. Carry sufficient water, sunscreen, insect repellent, and a hat. The park can get humid, so staying hydrated is essential.

- **Early Morning Visits:** For wildlife sightings, arrive early in the morning when animals are most active. Guided tours offer a more in-depth experience and enhance the chance of spotting various flora and fauna.

3. Planning a Day Trip to Elephanta Island

- **Ferry Schedule:** Ferries operate from the Gateway of India to Elephanta Island, with services running frequently from around 9:00 AM to 2:00 PM. Plan to catch an early ferry to give yourself ample time to explore the island and avoid the afternoon rush.

- **Physical Fitness:** The caves are located on a hill, accessible by a short but slightly steep uphill walk. Wearing comfortable shoes is recommended, and there are shaded resting spots and small vendors along the way to help make the climb easier.

- Food and Water: Elephanta Island has a few eateries, but they can be pricey and limited in options. Carrying some snacks and water will keep you energized and save time if you plan on a full day of exploration.

4. Water Sports and Boating Activities

- Check Weather Conditions: Many water sports in Mumbai are seasonal, typically operating from November to May when the seas are calm. Avoid water activities during the monsoon season (June to September) as rough waters can make these activities dangerous.

- Choosing Reputable Operators: If you plan to try jet skiing, parasailing, or other water sports, ensure you choose a reputable operator who provides safety equipment and is certified. Ask questions about their safety measures and look for recent customer reviews if possible.

- Safety Gear and Precautions: Always use the safety gear provided, follow the instructions of the operators, and ask about emergency procedures if you are unfamiliar with the activity. Some activities, like snorkeling, may require a bit of swimming knowledge, so it's best to be prepared.

5. General Tips for All Outdoor Activities

- Stay Hydrated: Mumbai's humid climate can lead to dehydration, especially if you're outdoors. Carry a reusable water bottle, ideally one with a filter, if you're planning an extended outdoor excursion.

- Respect Local Wildlife and Nature: In natural areas like Sanjay Gandhi National Park, avoid disturbing wildlife, and refrain from littering. If you're visiting beaches, leave no trace to help preserve the natural beauty of these spaces.

- Pack Essentials for Comfort: Sunscreen, sunglasses, a hat, and a light jacket are useful items to bring, as Mumbai's weather can vary. An umbrella is also handy, as sudden showers are common, especially during the monsoon season.

- Prepare for Traffic: Mumbai's traffic can make it challenging to reach destinations on time. Leave early, especially if you have ferry reservations or tours scheduled. Planning for traffic gives you more time to explore and less time stressing about delays.

These practical tips will ensure that your experience with Mumbai's nature and outdoor activities is smooth, enjoyable, and safe. Whether you're relaxing on the beach, exploring ancient caves, or trekking in lush forests, a little planning can go a long way toward making these adventures truly memorable.

Chapter 8

Nightlife and Entertainment

Mumbai is a city that truly comes alive after dark, offering a vibrant, eclectic nightlife that appeals to a wide range of tastes. From chic rooftop bars to theaters celebrating traditional art forms, Mumbai's nightlife promises memorable experiences for travelers and locals alike. This chapter will guide you through the best spots for entertainment, cultural performances, and nightlife safety tips to help you enjoy Mumbai responsibly.

Popular Nightclubs, Bars, and Lounges

Mumbai's nightlife scene is a blend of high-energy clubs, intimate lounges, and elegant bars that cater to every style. For those seeking a lively party vibe, nightclubs like Tryst in Lower Parel and Kitty Su at The Lalit hotel offer dance floors with a mix of EDM, Bollywood hits, and hip-hop tunes. Each club has its unique theme, with dazzling light shows and impressive sound systems that set the perfect mood.

For a more laid-back evening, Mumbai's upscale lounges are ideal. Social in multiple locations, including Colaba and Bandra, combines an industrial-chic ambiance with inventive cocktails, while Olive Bar & Kitchen in Khar is renowned for its Mediterranean-inspired drinks and stylish interiors. Lounges like Bonobo in Bandra bring together a relaxed crowd, featuring indie music and open-air settings, perfect for unwinding with friends.

Each location offers something unique, from high-octane parties to mellow gatherings. Dress codes can vary—some clubs are more relaxed, while upscale bars may require smart casual attire. Make sure to check the club or lounge's policy, as some venues are members-only or prioritize reservations.

Rooftop Bars and Sea-Facing Venues

Mumbai's rooftop bars and sea-facing venues are perfect for those who want to take in the city's skyline or enjoy the cool breeze of the Arabian Sea. Rooftop venues like Aer at the Four Seasons Hotel in Worli offer panoramic views of the city lights, accompanied by a well-curated menu of premium cocktails and wines. As one of the city's highest open-air bars, it's an excellent spot for a sundowner, where visitors can watch the city transition from day to night.

At Dome at the InterContinental Marine Drive, guests are treated to an upscale ambiance with sea views that capture the essence of Mumbai's coastal allure. With an array of fine wines, spirits, and signature cocktails, Dome is popular for romantic evenings and special occasions. Other favorites include Radio Bar in Bandra, which offers a quirky, retro vibe with music-inspired decor and creative cocktails.

For a taste of local flavor, head to Breeze in Powai, overlooking the Powai Lake, or Razzberry Rhinoceros in Juhu, where the serene sea backdrop pairs well with their fusion cuisine and extensive drink menu. These venues are perfect for a relaxed evening where conversation flows as freely as the drinks.

Cultural Performances and Theatres

Mumbai's cultural scene is deeply rooted in its history, with theaters and performance spaces that celebrate art in all its forms. Prithvi Theatre in Juhu, founded by the Kapoor family, is a hub for theater enthusiasts, showcasing everything from Hindi and English plays to poetry readings. Its intimate setting brings you close to the performers, creating a unique experience that's both authentic and engaging. The adjoining Prithvi Café is a great place to mingle with artists and locals over a cup of cutting chai.

The National Centre for the Performing Arts (NCPA) in Nariman Point is another cultural landmark, hosting a range of performances from classical music to contemporary dance and theater. Its multi-venue complex includes the Tata Theatre, Godrej Dance Theatre, and more, making it a vibrant space for cultural exchange.

Here, you can enjoy everything from Hindustani and Carnatic music concerts to ballet performances and film screenings.

Live music venues like The Royal Opera House and AntiSocial in Khar add another layer to Mumbai's music scene, featuring jazz nights, rock concerts, and indie music festivals. Check the venue schedules in advance, as shows often sell out, and purchasing tickets online can be more convenient. Mumbai's theaters and live music venues offer a blend of modern and traditional performances, bringing you closer to the soul of the city.

Tips for Staying Safe While Enjoying Mumbai's Nightlife

While Mumbai's nightlife is generally safe, it's wise to take precautions, especially when exploring the city at night. Here are some tips for a secure and enjoyable evening:

- Stick to Well-Known Venues: Mumbai has a variety of bars, clubs, and lounges, but it's best to choose reputable, well-reviewed locations. Established venues have safety protocols, reliable staff, and good crowd management.

- Transportation Tips: Avoid traveling alone late at night. Use trusted taxi services like Uber or Ola, which offer reliable rides and GPS tracking. Many venues also have designated cab stands nearby, or the concierge can arrange a safe ride for you.

- Drink Responsibly: Drink in moderation, and avoid accepting drinks from strangers. Many clubs offer "no questions asked" assistance if you feel unwell or unsafe, so don't hesitate to ask staff for help.

- Stay with Friends: Nightclubs and bars are best enjoyed with company. Staying with friends allows you to look out for each other, making the night safer and more enjoyable.

- **Carry Essential Items:** It's wise to carry a small bag with essentials like cash, ID, a phone charger, and a bottle of water. Keep your belongings close, as crowded venues can sometimes attract pickpockets.

- **Be Aware of Closing Times:** While some venues operate late into the night, it's helpful to know closing times in advance to plan your night. Clubs and bars generally close by 1:30 AM, with a few exceptions, so arrange transport accordingly.

With the city's rich nightlife and entertainment options, Mumbai offers an unforgettable experience. From lively clubs and serene rooftop bars to cultural performances and eclectic theaters, there's something for everyone. By following these practical tips, you'll be well-prepared to dive into Mumbai's vibrant night scene safely and enjoy every moment.

Chapter 9

Mumbai's Spiritual and Religious Sites

Mumbai's diverse spiritual and religious heritage is an essential part of the city's identity. From ancient Hindu temples and grand cathedrals to serene mosques and sacred shrines, these sites reflect the city's centuries-old ethos of tolerance and unity. Exploring Mumbai's spiritual sites provides travelers with a unique perspective on its history, culture, and the deep-seated traditions that unite its people.

Temples of Mumbai

Mumbai is home to several revered Hindu temples, each with its distinct history and atmosphere. One of the city's most famous temples is the Siddhivinayak Temple in Prabhadevi, dedicated to Lord Ganesha, the remover of obstacles. This temple draws thousands of devotees every Tuesday, considered an auspicious day for Ganesha worship. The temple's intricate wooden doors are adorned with carvings of Ashtavinayak (the eight forms of Ganesha), adding a touch of sacred artistry to the bustling environment. Visitors should arrive early to avoid crowds and observe the rituals that make this site so special.

Babulnath Temple, located on a hill near Girgaon, is one of the oldest temples in Mumbai, dedicated to Lord Shiva. The temple's quiet atmosphere and hilltop location offer a peaceful retreat from the city below, especially at dawn when worshippers arrive for morning prayers. Another iconic temple, Mumbadevi Temple, honors the city's namesake, Goddess Mumbadevi, the patron deity of the original fishing community of Mumbai. Nestled in the heart of the Zaveri Bazaar, the temple has stood as a symbol of the city's cultural roots since the 14th century.

Other notable temples include ISKCON Juhu, which showcases vibrant celebrations, especially during Janmashtami, and Walkeshwar Temple near Banganga Tank, said to be connected to the epic Ramayana. Each of these temples offers unique insights into the local culture and religious customs, and visitors are encouraged to dress modestly and respect the sanctity of these spaces.

Churches and Cathedrals

Mumbai's colonial past has left a lasting legacy of magnificent churches and cathedrals, serving as both places of worship and architectural marvels. St. Thomas Cathedral, built in 1718, is the oldest Anglican church in Mumbai and is located in the historic Fort area. Its simple yet elegant structure features Gothic arches, stained glass windows, and a tranquil interior, making it a peaceful spot amidst the city's financial district. The cathedral's history reflects the city's colonial heritage, with memorial plaques and inscriptions honoring British officers and early settlers.

On Bandra Hill, the Basilica of Our Lady of the Mount, known as Mount Mary Church, is a beloved site for both Catholics and people of other faiths. The basilica is renowned for its annual Bandra Fair, held in September, which attracts pilgrims from across India. The church's Portuguese-style architecture, combined with its picturesque location overlooking the Arabian Sea, adds to its serene atmosphere. Pilgrims come here to pray to Mother Mary, seeking blessings for health and peace. Visitors should be mindful of the local customs, especially during masses and special services, which are sacred moments for the church community.

Another noteworthy church is the Afghan Church in Colaba, built to commemorate soldiers who died in the First Afghan War. Its unique architecture and peaceful garden setting make it a hidden gem in Mumbai's southern district. Exploring these churches offers a glimpse into the city's rich Christian heritage and the deep devotion of the local Catholic community.

Mosques and Shrines

Mumbai's Islamic heritage is beautifully represented by its mosques and dargahs (shrines), which attract worshippers and tourists alike. The Haji Ali Dargah, one of the city's most iconic landmarks, is situated on a small islet off the coast of Worli. Built in memory of the Sufi saint Pir Haji Ali Shah Bukhari in the 15th century, the dargah is an architectural marvel with intricate marble latticework. During high tide, the narrow causeway leading to the dargah is submerged, giving the shrine an ethereal "floating" appearance. Visitors of all faiths are welcome, but it's important to dress modestly and be prepared to walk barefoot inside the shrine.

The Mahim Dargah, located in the Mahim area, is another significant religious site dedicated to Makhdum Ali Mahimi, a revered Sufi saint. Established in the 14th century, this dargah is an important center of Islamic learning and Sufi culture in Mumbai. The annual Urs festival, marking the saint's death anniversary, draws large crowds and offers a glimpse into the city's Islamic traditions. Visiting these dargahs allows travelers to experience the rich spiritual atmosphere that these sites preserve.

For those interested in Mumbai's Islamic architecture and Sufi traditions, both Haji Ali and Mahim Dargah provide a chance to observe the rituals and customs that define this religious heritage. Remember to check the prayer timings if you wish to experience the dargahs at their most vibrant.

Multi-Faith Harmony: Experiencing Mumbai's Religious Diversity

Mumbai is celebrated for its spirit of multi-faith harmony, with different religious communities coexisting peacefully. Walking through the city, it's common to find Hindu temples, mosques, churches, and even Jain temples and Zoroastrian fire temples within close proximity. This coexistence is a reflection of Mumbai's open-hearted nature, where faith is respected across lines of religion and caste.

MUMBAI TRAVEL GUIDE 2025

One of the city's remarkable examples of religious diversity is the Banganga Tank in Walkeshwar, an ancient water tank surrounded by Hindu temples, but often visited by people of various faiths for its tranquil ambiance. The Global Vipassana Pagoda near Gorai Beach is another site where people from all backgrounds come to meditate, drawn by the universal message of peace and mindfulness.

Travelers interested in understanding this multi-faith dimension can participate in festivals like Diwali, Eid, Christmas, and Ganesh Chaturthi. Each festival brings unique customs, decorations, and public celebrations, providing insight into the city's vibrant cultural tapestry. Experiencing these events can deepen one's appreciation for Mumbai's religious tolerance and community spirit.

Mumbai's spiritual and religious sites are more than just places of worship—they're living testaments to the city's diverse cultural and religious landscape. Exploring these temples, churches, mosques, and multi-faith traditions allows travelers to experience Mumbai's unique harmony, where every belief is woven into the fabric of daily life.

Practical Tips and Travel Guide Tips

Visiting Mumbai's spiritual sites can be an enriching experience, but some preparation and practical knowledge will enhance your visit. Here are some essential tips to help you make the most of your journey through these places of worship:

1. Dress Modestly and Respect Local Customs

- Many of Mumbai's temples, mosques, and churches have guidelines for modest attire. As a general rule, wear clothing that covers your shoulders, arms, and legs. This applies especially to temples and mosques, where traditional and modest dress is a sign of respect.

- At some sites, particularly in mosques and dargahs like Haji Ali, you may be required to cover your head. Carrying a scarf or shawl can be useful for this purpose.
- Be prepared to remove your shoes before entering temples and mosques. It's wise to wear shoes that are easy to slip on and off, especially if you plan on visiting multiple sites.

2. Plan Visits Around Worship Hours and Festivals

- Religious sites can be very crowded during prayer times and festivals, which can enhance the experience or make it overwhelming, depending on your preference.
- Visiting during early morning hours or on weekdays is often less crowded, allowing for a quieter experience and a chance to observe rituals more intimately.
- Ganesh Chaturthi and other major festivals draw thousands of visitors to places like Siddhivinayak Temple and Mount Mary Church. If you want to experience these celebrations, arrive early and be prepared for large crowds.

3. Observe Photography Rules

- Not all spiritual sites permit photography, particularly inside sanctuaries or near idols and religious icons. Check the rules before taking photos or videos.
- In some locations, such as the Haji Ali Dargah, photography may be restricted entirely. Look for signs or ask attendants to avoid causing disruption.
- If photography is allowed, consider being discreet and respectful, especially during worship or prayer times.

4. Carry Cash for Offerings and Entry Fees

- Many temples and mosques have donation boxes where visitors can offer small donations, a traditional practice that contributes to the maintenance of the site. Bringing small denominations is helpful for this purpose.

- Some larger sites, like the Elephanta Caves, may have small entry fees, especially for foreign visitors. While not always the case for religious sites, having cash on hand ensures you're prepared.

- You may also encounter vendors selling flowers, candles, or incense sticks outside many temples. These items can be used as offerings, and purchasing them helps support local artisans and vendors.

5. Book Guided Tours for Insightful Experiences

- Certain religious sites offer guided tours, often through private guides or agencies. Tours of places like Mahim Dargah or Siddhivinayak Temple can provide deeper insights into their history, architecture, and cultural significance.

- Local tour guides, especially for multi-faith explorations, can offer valuable context on Mumbai's religious diversity. Guided experiences are especially helpful in areas like Dharavi, where ethical and knowledgeable guides ensure a respectful and informative experience.

6. Mind Your Belongings and Stay Aware of Crowds

- Large gatherings during festivals or prayer times can attract crowds, so keep your belongings secure, especially in busy places like Haji Ali and Mount Mary during peak times.

- Avoid carrying large bags inside spiritual sites. Many places have storage areas, but carrying only essentials is generally easier and allows you to move around comfortably.

7. Experience Multi-Faith Diversity with Respect

- Mumbai's religious sites are a symbol of the city's unique multi-faith identity. Visiting temples, churches, and mosques in close succession can give you a richer appreciation for Mumbai's inclusivity.

- Engage respectfully with worshippers if they're open to conversation. Many locals are proud of their traditions and are happy to share stories or rituals with visitors. A simple greeting and genuine curiosity can go a long way.

8. Timing and Tide Considerations for Haji Ali Dargah

- The causeway leading to Haji Ali Dargah is only accessible during low tide. Check local tide schedules to avoid being stranded or unable to access the dargah.

- During monsoon season (June to September), the causeway may be closed due to high tides and rough seas. Plan accordingly if visiting during this period.

9. Take Advantage of Audio Guides and Mobile Apps

- Many popular religious sites now offer audio guides or apps that provide historical and cultural context. This can be particularly helpful at places like St. Thomas Cathedral or ISKCON Juhu, where history and architecture play a key role.

- Audio guides allow for a self-paced visit and offer flexibility in exploring the site on your terms.

10. Be Mindful of Quiet Zones and Sacred Spaces

- Many religious sites have areas designated for quiet meditation or prayer. Respect the silence, and avoid loud conversations or disturbances in these spaces.

- If you're unfamiliar with the rituals, observe quietly and follow the lead of local worshippers. Some customs may involve gestures, offerings, or forms of greeting that are unique to each site.

By observing these tips, you'll ensure a respectful and fulfilling visit to Mumbai's spiritual and religious sites, gaining insights into the city's unique religious diversity. Each location provides a meaningful connection to Mumbai's soul, offering experiences that are both introspective and enriching.

Chapter 10

Family-Friendly Activities

Mumbai is a vibrant city that caters wonderfully to families, offering a blend of educational experiences, entertaining attractions, and scenic spots perfect for a family day out. From aquariums and planetariums to spacious beaches and engaging cultural hubs, Mumbai has options to keep both young and older family members entertained. This guide explores the best family-friendly spots in the city, ensuring memorable and enjoyable experiences for all ages.

Kid-Friendly Attractions

- Taraporewala Aquarium

Located along Marine Drive, the Taraporewala Aquarium is one of Mumbai's longest-standing marine attractions, and it's a fantastic choice for children fascinated by underwater life. The aquarium houses an array of marine and freshwater species, from colorful fish to coral and other sea creatures. Inside, children can observe the marine world up close, learning about different aquatic species and their habitats. To make the most of this experience, consider visiting during weekdays when crowds are thinner, allowing for a more relaxed exploration.

- Nehru Planetarium

The Nehru Planetarium offers a captivating experience for children interested in astronomy. Located in Worli, the planetarium presents regular shows on space, the solar system, and beyond. Shows are conducted in multiple languages, including Hindi and English, making it accessible to a broad audience. The adjoining Nehru Science Center adds an extra layer of engagement, featuring interactive exhibits that cover topics like physics, chemistry, and biology. This makes it an ideal spot for a family outing with both educational and entertainment value. Arrive early, as shows tend to be popular and tickets can sell out quickly.

- KidZania Mumbai

A unique attraction located in R-City Mall, KidZania Mumbai is a miniature city designed specifically for children, where they can try out various roles and professions in a safe, interactive environment. Children can experience being doctors, firefighters, pilots, or chefs, complete with uniforms and tasks that mirror the real world. The activities are immersive and guided, promoting learning through play, creativity, and social skills. KidZania also has areas dedicated to toddlers, making it a suitable attraction for families with younger children. This indoor park is an all-weather activity, ideal during Mumbai's rainy season.

Family Beaches and Picnic Spots

- Juhu Beach

One of Mumbai's most iconic beaches, Juhu Beach offers a lively atmosphere for families. Kids can play in the sand, splash in the waves, and enjoy a variety of local snacks like bhel puri and vada pav sold by beachside vendors. The beach is especially enjoyable in the early morning when it's quieter, or in the late afternoon, as the sun sets and families and vendors gather for a relaxed evening by the sea.

- Sanjay Gandhi National Park (SGNP)

This vast national park on the northern outskirts of Mumbai is an excellent spot for a family outing. SGNP has a rich ecosystem of flora and fauna, along with attractions such as the Kanheri Caves, boating, and lion and tiger safaris. A small toy train, the Van Rani, operates within the park and is popular with young children. The park also offers various trails, ranging from beginner to advanced, allowing families to enjoy a bit of trekking in a safe environment.

Packing a picnic to enjoy in the designated picnic areas can make this day-long outing even more memorable.

- Hanging Gardens and Kamala Nehru Park

Located on Malabar Hill, the Hanging Gardens and Kamala Nehru Park are beautifully maintained green spaces that offer a peaceful escape from Mumbai's bustling streets. The gardens overlook Marine Drive, providing panoramic views of the Arabian Sea and the city skyline. Kamala Nehru Park has play areas for children, including a giant shoe structure that kids love to climb. Both parks are ideal for a relaxed family afternoon, with ample shaded spots for picnics.

Cultural and Educational Experiences for Families

- Chhatrapati Shivaji Maharaj Vastu Sangrahalaya (CSMVS)

For families interested in history, art, and culture, the CSMVS museum in South Mumbai offers an impressive collection of artifacts, sculptures, and art from India's rich cultural heritage. The museum has dedicated programs and workshops for children, making it an interactive learning experience. For families with older children, guided tours can provide an educational journey through India's history and traditions.

- Mani Bhavan Gandhi Sangrahalaya

This small yet significant museum, once the residence of Mahatma Gandhi, provides insight into the life and legacy of the Mahatma. The museum includes a library, a photo gallery, and dioramas that depict scenes from Gandhi's life, such as the Dandi March. It's a thought-provoking place to visit for families, especially those with school-age children who are curious about India's history and the figures who shaped it.

- Dr. Bhau Daji Lad Museum

This museum, located in Byculla, is Mumbai's oldest museum and houses collections that showcase Mumbai's evolution and history. The museum often hosts workshops, storytelling sessions, and exhibitions tailored for young audiences, making it both fun and educational for families. The museum building itself is a piece of art, with intricate interiors and architecture that transport visitors back in time.

Safety Tips for Traveling with Kids in Mumbai

- Stay Hydrated and Sun-Protected

    Mumbai can be hot and humid, so ensure that you and your children stay hydrated throughout the day. Carry reusable water bottles, sunscreen, hats, and sunglasses, especially if you're exploring outdoor attractions like Juhu Beach or SGNP.

- Keep Essentials Handy

    Carry essentials like hand sanitizer, wet wipes, and light snacks. Traffic and queues are common in Mumbai, so having small snacks can keep younger kids content while you wait. It's also wise to have a portable first-aid kit for minor scrapes or insect bites.

- Use Registered Transport and Be Cautious on Roads

    Stick to registered taxis, ride-hailing services, or the city's efficient train system to get around safely. Mumbai's traffic can be hectic, so ensure that children stay close, particularly when navigating crowded areas or crossing streets.

- Be Mindful of Personal Belongings

    Mumbai is generally safe, but crowded markets and popular attractions can attract pickpockets. Keep an eye on your belongings, especially in busy places like street markets and popular beach areas. Consider using a secure backpack with zippers for added safety.

- Follow Safety Guidelines at Beaches and Parks

    While Mumbai's beaches are beautiful, the tides can be unpredictable. Be cautious about swimming, and avoid the water during monsoon season. Similarly, if trekking in SGNP, stick to marked trails and avoid secluded areas, as wildlife like monkeys and small reptiles can be present.

Mumbai offers a multitude of family-friendly activities that are both fun and educational, making it an ideal destination for parents and children alike. With the right planning, families can discover the city's unique blend of nature, culture, and entertainment while creating memories that last a lifetime.

Practical Tips and Travel Guide Tips

Traveling with family, especially with kids, requires a bit more planning and preparation. Here are some valuable tips to ensure a smooth and enjoyable experience while exploring family-friendly attractions in Mumbai:

Planning Your Itinerary

1. Prioritize Key Attractions

    With so much to see in Mumbai, plan your itinerary based on your children's interests and energy levels. Start with high-energy activities like KidZania or the planetarium earlier in the day and leave more relaxed attractions, such as Juhu Beach or a park visit, for later in the afternoon. This pacing helps prevent children from becoming overtired.

2. Check Show and Opening Times

    Some attractions, like the Nehru Planetarium and KidZania, have scheduled showtimes and peak hours, so check ahead and book tickets online if available. The Nehru Planetarium, for instance, has specific show timings that can fill up quickly, so planning ahead ensures you won't miss out.

3. Plan Around Traffic

    Mumbai's traffic can be a challenge, especially during peak hours (8–11 AM and 5–8 PM). Try to plan activities within the same area for the day to minimize travel time. For instance, if you're visiting the aquarium, explore nearby Marine Drive and Colaba for a convenient day out.

Keeping Kids Engaged and Comfortable

1. Encourage Curiosity

    Many of Mumbai's attractions, like the CSMVS museum and planetarium, provide fascinating educational experiences for children. Encourage their curiosity by preparing them with a little background about what they'll see and asking them questions along the way.

2. Pack Smart

    Mumbai's warm weather calls for essentials like sunscreen, hats, and sunglasses, as well as light clothing. Having a bag stocked with snacks, wipes, and water bottles is also essential, as children might get hungry or thirsty frequently during outdoor activities. Keep hand sanitizer handy as well, especially after street food adventures.

3. Bring Strollers or Baby Carriers

    If you're traveling with toddlers, a stroller or baby carrier can make a big difference in comfort and convenience, especially at places like the Hanging Gardens or Colaba Causeway. These attractions involve a fair amount of walking, and a stroller can give little ones a chance to rest.

Eating Out with Kids

1. Look for Child-Friendly Restaurants

    While Mumbai has a fantastic array of restaurants, not all may be child-friendly. Restaurants around tourist areas or malls, like those near Juhu Beach or R-City Mall, often cater to families and have menu options suited for kids. KidZania also has food options on-site, making it convenient for a day-long outing.

2. Street Food Safety

Mumbai's street food is an experience, but for children, it's best to exercise caution. Stick to busy vendors and try cooked dishes like pav bhaji or freshly made vada pav. Avoid foods like raw salads or pani puri from lesser-known vendors to reduce the risk of digestive issues. Opt for coconut water or bottled water to keep everyone hydrated safely.

Navigating Busy Spots and Staying Safe

1. Use Child Identification and Safety Tips

In crowded areas like markets or popular beaches, it's easy for children to get lost in the crowd. Consider giving kids a small card with your contact information in case of separation. Make sure they know what to do if they get lost and remind them to stay close at all times.

2. Choose Family-Friendly Accommodation

Many Mumbai hotels offer family-friendly amenities like swimming pools, kids' play areas, or babysitting services. Opting for a centrally located hotel can save you travel time and make it easier to return for midday breaks, especially if you're exploring busy areas like Colaba or Juhu.

3. Stay Aware of Weather Conditions

Mumbai can be quite humid, and the monsoon season (June to September) brings heavy rainfall. If you're traveling during this time, plan for mostly indoor activities or choose spots like KidZania or museums that don't depend on outdoor weather. During the summer, plan beach visits for the early morning or late afternoon to avoid the midday sun.

4. Prepare for Wildlife in Outdoor Locations

At outdoor spots like Sanjay Gandhi National Park, it's common to encounter monkeys, birds, and other wildlife. Teach children to observe animals from a distance and avoid feeding them, as this can be unsafe. Carry insect repellent if you're planning to spend extended time in parks or forested areas to keep mosquitoes at bay.

Making the Most of Family Attractions

1. Engage with Local Guides

    Many of Mumbai's popular attractions, such as the CSMVS museum and Elephanta Island, offer guided tours. These tours are often educational and can engage children with interesting stories about Mumbai's history and culture, adding depth to their experience.

2. Participate in Interactive Experiences

    Many places, including the Nehru Planetarium and KidZania, offer interactive learning. If possible, book hands-on activities, such as a workshop at a museum or a simulated role-play activity at KidZania, to keep kids actively involved and learning.

3. Photography and Souvenirs

    Kids often enjoy capturing memories, so encourage them to bring along a simple camera or a notebook for sketching or taking notes about the places they visit. Look for small souvenirs at street markets like Colaba Causeway or Crawford Market; kids will love picking out local handicrafts or trinkets as keepsakes.

These practical tips can help you enjoy a smooth, stress-free family adventure in Mumbai, allowing everyone to experience the city's vibrant energy, unique attractions, and cultural richness. With a bit of planning and flexibility, your family can create unforgettable memories in the heart of Mumbai.

Chapter 11

Mumbai for the Adventurous Traveler

Mumbai offers more than its iconic landmarks and beaches—beneath the surface, there's an energetic, adventurous side of the city that beckons thrill-seekers and urban explorers alike. From offbeat locations and graffiti-covered streets to scenic trekking trails and adrenaline-pumping water sports, Mumbai has a lot to offer those with an appetite for discovery. This chapter delves into some of the most exciting, less-explored corners of the city and surrounding areas, designed to fuel your adventurous spirit.

Urban Exploring: Offbeat Locations, Graffiti Spots, and Unique Finds

For those interested in the city's underground culture and urban art scene, Mumbai holds hidden gems and vibrant art spaces that are a far cry from the usual tourist circuit.

1. Bandra's Graffiti Alley

    The neighborhood of Bandra, particularly around Chapel Road and St. Peter's Church, is an art lover's paradise. Known for its colorful street murals and thought-provoking graffiti, this area showcases works by local and international artists, providing a powerful glimpse into the city's urban culture. As you walk through the lanes, you'll encounter murals that touch on social themes, quirky portraits, and abstract expressions—perfect for photography enthusiasts.

2. Dharavi's Art Spaces and Pottery Village

    Beyond its reputation as Asia's largest slum, Dharavi has a vibrant arts and craft community. You'll find a pottery village here where traditional artisans create intricate clay wares, giving visitors a unique look at local craftsmanship. Additionally, some sections of Dharavi have been transformed with street art, thanks to various community-driven initiatives. Join a guided tour to better understand the social context and creative energy of this thriving community.

3. Exploring Byculla's Lost Spaces

    Byculla's old mills and forgotten buildings echo the industrial past of Mumbai. Some of these historic structures have now become unconventional spots for photographers and explorers. From crumbling walls to vintage architecture, Byculla offers an eerie, yet fascinating, glimpse into a bygone era. Be sure to go with a guide familiar with the area, as some spots may require permission to enter.

Trekking Trails: Kanheri Caves, Yeoor Hills, and Nearby Destinations

Mumbai's proximity to the Western Ghats means there are scenic trekking trails within and around the city, perfect for a quick adventure in nature.

1. Kanheri Caves

    Located within Sanjay Gandhi National Park, the ancient Kanheri Caves combine history with nature. A short trek through dense forest brings you to this complex of Buddhist caves, many of which date back to the first century. The hike itself is moderate and leads you through lush landscapes teeming with local wildlife. The reward at the top is panoramic views of the park and the city, as well as a serene atmosphere within the historic caves.

2. Yeoor Hills

   Yeoor Hills, part of the Thane region, offers an escape from Mumbai's urban chaos and a quieter trek with scenic trails. Known for its green cover, wildlife, and occasional waterfalls during the monsoon, Yeoor is ideal for early-morning treks. Local guides often lead nature walks here, explaining the area's rich biodiversity and pointing out interesting flora and fauna along the way.

3. Matheran and Rajmachi Fort

   For those seeking a day trip, Matheran and Rajmachi Fort are both popular trekking destinations accessible within a few hours from Mumbai. Matheran's red-soil trails and viewpoints are a delight to explore, especially since no vehicles are allowed in the area. Rajmachi Fort offers a more challenging trek, with an uphill trail leading to a historic fort and breathtaking valley views, particularly beautiful in the monsoon season.

Scuba Diving, Paragliding, and Other Thrilling Adventures

For thrill-seekers who crave action-packed experiences, Mumbai and its nearby regions don't disappoint. From diving below the surface to gliding over scenic landscapes, you'll find plenty of ways to get your adrenaline fix.

1. Scuba Diving in Malvan

   Although not directly in Mumbai, Malvan is a popular diving destination a few hours away. Here, the clear Arabian Sea waters allow you to explore vibrant coral reefs, colorful fish, and intriguing underwater landscapes. Several operators in Mumbai offer scuba diving excursions, including travel arrangements to Malvan, complete with certified instructors and equipment.

2. Paragliding in Kamshet

    Just a few hours from Mumbai, Kamshet is one of India's premier paragliding destinations. The rolling Sahyadri hills and open skies make for an incredible flying experience. Paragliding schools in the area offer tandem flights with experienced instructors, making it accessible for beginners and thrill-seekers alike. For the best experience, visit between October and May, when weather conditions are optimal for paragliding.

3. Jet Skiing and Boating in Alibaug

    If you prefer watersports closer to Mumbai, Alibaug offers jet skiing, banana boat rides, and kayaking along its beaches. This coastal town is a ferry ride away from the city and is perfect for a weekend getaway packed with adventure activities. You'll find instructors and rental services on Alibaug's popular beaches, ensuring a safe and exciting experience.

Exploring the Local Night Markets and Late-Night Food Scenes

Mumbai's bustling night markets and late-night food culture offer a lively end to a day of exploration, ideal for night owls and food lovers who enjoy the city's unique flavors and atmospheres.

1. Colaba Causeway

    Colaba Causeway, one of Mumbai's most famous shopping streets, stays lively into the night. Here, you can browse through jewelry, antiques, and handicrafts before stopping for a bite at Leopold Café or Café Mondegar, two historic eateries beloved by locals and visitors alike. The energy and eclectic mix of people make it a must-see, even if you're just here to people-watch.

2. Juhu Beach Food Stalls

   Juhu Beach comes alive in the evening with a lineup of street vendors serving delicious local favorites like pav bhaji, bhel puri, and gola (flavored ice treats). The beach is filled with families, tourists, and locals enjoying the cool sea breeze and tasty snacks. Be prepared for crowds and take in the vibrant sounds and sights as you sample Mumbai's iconic street food.

3. Mohammed Ali Road During Ramadan

   For a unique culinary adventure, head to Mohammed Ali Road during the holy month of Ramadan. This area transforms into a bustling food haven at night, with vendors offering an incredible variety of kebabs, sweets, and biryanis. From melt-in-your-mouth mutton seekh kebabs to the rich malpua dessert, you'll find a host of culinary treasures here. Be prepared for crowds, but know that the experience is well worth it.

4. Late-Night Food Spots: Kayani & Co. and Bade Miya
   Mumbai is known for its all-hours dining culture. Bade Miya in Colaba is a late-night institution, serving kebabs, rolls, and biryanis well past midnight. For a different vibe, try Kayani & Co. in South Mumbai, where you can savor Irani-style bun maska (bread with butter) and chai late into the night. These places embody the spirit of Mumbai's food scene and are perfect for a memorable, satisfying end to an adventurous day.

Mumbai's adventurous side has something for everyone, whether you're exploring graffiti-laden alleys, trekking through natural reserves, diving into the Arabian Sea, or savoring the lively late-night food scene. With these experiences, you're sure to gain a deeper, more thrilling perspective on this dynamic city. Prepare for a journey full of unexpected discoveries, adrenaline-fueled activities, and unforgettable memories in the heart of Mumbai.

Chapter 12

Practical Travel Information

When planning a trip to Mumbai, having reliable information on essentials like visa requirements, currency exchange, and mobile connectivity can make a big difference in your experience. This chapter provides comprehensive details on these fundamental aspects, so you're prepared and well-equipped for a smooth journey.

Travel Essentials: Visa, Currency Exchange, and Mobile Connectivity

Mumbai's rich culture, bustling city life, and countless attractions draw visitors from around the world. To make the most of your trip, it's crucial to have your travel documents in order, access to local currency, and an easy way to stay connected. Here, we cover the essentials for a seamless travel experience.

Visa Requirements and Tips

India requires most international visitors to obtain a visa before entry. However, the type of visa, application process, and duration of stay depend on your nationality and the purpose of your visit. Here are the common types of visas available for travelers heading to Mumbai:

1. e-Visa
   Many nationalities are eligible for India's e-Visa, which can be applied for online through the official Indian government website. The e-Visa is a convenient option, covering various types, including tourist, business, and medical purposes.

- Duration: The tourist e-Visa typically grants stays of 30 days, 1 year, or even 5 years, depending on the selected option.
- Application Process: Complete the online application, submit necessary documents (such as a passport copy and recent photo), and pay the fee. Processing usually takes 3-5 business days.
- Important Note: Ensure that your passport has at least six months' validity and two blank pages.

2. Regular Visa

For longer stays or multi-entry purposes, you may need a regular tourist visa, which requires an application at an Indian consulate or embassy.

- Duration: Typically available for six months to one year.
- Application Process: Visit the nearest Indian consulate or embassy to complete the application and provide supporting documents, including proof of travel plans and financial means.

3. Visa Extensions and Conversions

Extensions for e-Visas are generally not permitted, so ensure your selected visa covers your planned stay. Regular visa holders can request extensions through the Foreigners Regional Registration Office (FRRO) in India, but approvals can vary.

Tip: Keep both physical and digital copies of your visa, passport, and other important documents. It's advisable to save them in a secure cloud storage or mobile app for easy access in case of emergencies.

Currency Exchange and Banking Tips

The Indian Rupee (INR) is the official currency, and you'll need local currency for day-to-day expenses. Although credit cards are widely accepted in Mumbai's hotels, malls, and larger restaurants, cash is essential for small vendors, taxis, and street food stalls.

1. Currency Exchange Options

    o Airport Exchanges: Mumbai's Chhatrapati Shivaji Maharaj International Airport has several currency exchange counters in both arrivals and departures, though rates are generally less favorable.

    o Banks and ATMs: Major banks offer competitive exchange rates and can be found throughout the city. ATMs are widespread in Mumbai, allowing you to withdraw rupees with international cards. Check with your bank regarding foreign transaction fees.

    o Exchange Bureaus: Exchange bureaus in popular tourist areas like Colaba and Bandra often provide better rates than airports. Ensure they are authorized and offer a receipt.

2. Using Credit Cards and Digital Payments
Mumbai is rapidly adopting digital payments, especially through platforms like Paytm, Google Pay, and PhonePe. These options are widely used for retail, dining, and transportation.

    o Credit Cards: Visa, MasterCard, and American Express are accepted at most high-end establishments. Carry some cash for smaller merchants that may not accept cards.

    o Digital Wallets: Consider downloading a local e-wallet app if you plan to stay for a while, as these are convenient for payments at smaller shops, restaurants, and even local transportation services.

Tip: It's helpful to carry a mix of cash and digital payment options. Mumbai can be a cash-centric city, so keep small bills on hand, especially for places like street markets and auto-rickshaws.

Mobile Connectivity and Internet Access

Staying connected in Mumbai is relatively easy with the range of mobile and internet options available. Local SIM cards are widely accessible and affordable, giving you reliable mobile service and data throughout the city.

1. Purchasing a Local SIM Card

    The main telecom providers in Mumbai include Jio, Airtel, and Vodafone-Idea. All three offer prepaid plans for data, voice, and SMS services.

    - Airport and Retail Stores: You can purchase a SIM card at the airport on arrival or at retail stores in the city. Bring a copy of your passport, visa, and a passport-sized photo, as these documents are required to register your SIM.
    - Choosing a Plan: Prepaid plans are flexible and usually range from a few days to several months. Plans often include unlimited local calls and high-speed data, so pick one that fits your anticipated usage.

2. Data and Internet Coverage

    Mumbai offers excellent mobile data coverage across the city, and most areas have 4G LTE connectivity. Telecom providers also offer packages for international roaming if you prefer to use your own SIM card, but this is typically more expensive than purchasing a local one.

    - Public Wi-Fi: While many cafes, hotels, and malls provide free Wi-Fi, connections may not be as secure or stable as mobile data. If reliable internet is a priority, consider a plan with adequate data for your needs.

3. Downloading Essential Apps

    A few essential apps will enhance your travel experience in Mumbai:

    - Transportation: Download Uber, Ola, or Rapido for easy and reliable rides.
    - Digital Payments: Paytm, Google Pay, or PhonePe are widely used for digital transactions.
    - Translation: Google Translate can help with basic Hindi phrases and interactions.

- Local Reviews: Zomato or Swiggy (for food) and Justdial for local services can make navigation easier.

Tip: For added security, consider using a virtual private network (VPN) while connecting to public Wi-Fi networks, as this will help protect your personal information.

With this guide to the essentials of travel in Mumbai, you're ready to handle the practical side of your trip smoothly. Equipped with the right visa, access to local currency, and reliable connectivity, you'll be well-prepared to focus on the city's experiences and enjoy all that Mumbai has to offer.

Staying Safe in Mumbai: Tips on Health, Safety, and Avoiding Scams

Mumbai is generally a safe city, yet, as with any bustling metropolis, there are a few practical measures to keep in mind to ensure a smooth, trouble-free journey. Here's a guide to staying healthy, secure, and scam-aware as you explore the city.

1. Health Precautions
   Staying healthy while traveling begins with preventive care. Mumbai's warm, humid climate and urban environment can pose a few challenges, so keep these tips in mind:
   - Hydrate and Protect from Heat: Mumbai's tropical climate can be demanding, especially during summer. Make sure to stay hydrated and wear light, breathable clothing. Sunscreen and a hat are must-haves for daytime excursions.
   - Street Food Safety: Mumbai's street food is delicious and a big part of the local culture. However, be mindful of where and what you eat. Opt for stalls that are busy (a sign of fresh turnover), and

avoid uncooked foods like salads or chutneys that may be washed with tap water.

- Tap Water and Hygiene: Avoid drinking tap water. Instead, buy bottled or filtered water, which is readily available throughout the city. Be mindful of ice cubes in drinks, which may not be made from purified water.

- Vaccinations and Preventive Medications: Check with your healthcare provider on recommended vaccinations before visiting Mumbai. Consider medications for mosquito-borne diseases if you plan to explore areas near water or greenery.

2. Personal Safety and Common Scams

Mumbai is known for its vibrant crowds and active nightlife, but like any major tourist destination, it has its share of petty crime and scams.

- Avoiding Pickpockets: Keep your belongings close, particularly in crowded areas like train stations, markets, and tourist hotspots. Carry a secure, zippered bag and avoid displaying valuable items.

- Common Tourist Scams: Be cautious of overly persistent vendors, unofficial "tour guides," and individuals offering unsolicited assistance. Some common scams include inflated prices for taxi rides (always use the meter or a ride-hailing app), fake ticket sellers, and vendors who offer products and then charge excessive prices after.

- Safe Transportation: Stick to recognized transportation options. For taxis, insist on using the meter or opt for trusted ride-sharing apps like Uber and Ola, which offer transparency and reliability.

3. Night Safety

Mumbai is lively at night, with popular spots staying open late. While the city is generally safe after dark, exercise caution as you would in any urban environment.

- o Stick to Well-Lit Areas: If exploring at night, stick to well-lit, crowded areas and avoid deserted lanes.

- o Plan Your Transportation: Pre-arrange your transportation back to your hotel. Late-night travel is best done with trusted ride services.

- o Stay in Groups When Possible: Solo travelers can have a wonderful time in Mumbai, but for nighttime activities, it's often safer (and more enjoyable) to go with friends or other travelers.

Pro Tip: When taking photos or using your phone in public, keep a close grip on your belongings, especially in crowded areas where bag snatchers may be active.

Navigating Medical Services and Pharmacies

Whether you're in need of a minor medical remedy or something more extensive, Mumbai has a wide range of medical facilities, pharmacies, and hospitals that cater to both locals and visitors. Here's what you should know about accessing healthcare in the city.

1. Medical Services and Hospitals

    Mumbai is home to some of India's best hospitals, and healthcare facilities range from small clinics to multi-specialty hospitals with English-speaking staff. Many major hospitals in the city are accustomed to treating international patients, offering everything from general check-ups to emergency care.

    - o Major Hospitals: Popular hospitals for travelers include Bombay Hospital, Lilavati Hospital, Jaslok Hospital, and Kokilaben Dhirubhai Ambani Hospital. These institutions have high standards of care and 24-hour emergency services.

- Clinics and Smaller Medical Centers: For minor issues, numerous small clinics and doctor's offices are scattered across the city. Most hotels and locals can recommend a trusted clinic nearby.
- Emergency Services: The emergency contact number for ambulance services in Mumbai is 108. Most hospitals operate 24/7 emergency rooms. If you're not fluent in Hindi or Marathi, seeking help in major hospitals is best, as they are more likely to have English-speaking staff.

Pro Tip: It's useful to have a small first-aid kit on hand, especially if you plan to explore remote areas around Mumbai where immediate medical care may be less accessible.

2. Pharmacies and Access to Medication

Pharmacies, known locally as "medical stores," are easy to find in Mumbai, with many operating 24/7. They offer both over-the-counter and prescription medications, though some drugs commonly available elsewhere may require a prescription in India.

- Locating a Pharmacy: Pharmacies are abundant and often marked with a green cross sign. In areas like Colaba, Bandra, and Juhu, you'll find several open round-the-clock.
- Common Over-the-Counter Medications: Medications for headaches, colds, digestive issues, and minor cuts and bruises are available over the counter. Brands may differ from those back home, so ask for assistance if you're unsure of a specific product.
- Travel Insurance and Prescription Medications: If you're carrying prescription medications, bring a copy of your prescription with you. For those who require prescription refills during their stay, private hospitals and clinics can assist, though having travel insurance that covers medical costs is highly recommended.

3. Handling Medical Emergencies

   In case of a medical emergency, head to the nearest major hospital or call the national emergency number (108). Major hospitals in Mumbai are equipped to handle a wide range of emergencies and are accustomed to treating foreign nationals.

   - Language Barrier Tips: Although English is widely understood in medical facilities, having basic medical terms saved in your phone in Hindi can be helpful, especially in smaller clinics.

Pro Tip: Download an offline map of Mumbai and save emergency contact numbers, including those for your country's embassy or consulate, in case of an unexpected situation.

Mumbai's vibrant lifestyle and diversity offer travelers an unforgettable experience, and understanding the practicalities of staying healthy and safe will help ensure that your trip is smooth and enjoyable. By taking preventive measures, familiarizing yourself with the city's healthcare resources, and remaining aware of your surroundings, you'll be ready to explore Mumbai with confidence.

Chapter 13

Insider Tips and Local Insights

Discovering Mumbai's spirit means looking beyond its popular tourist spots and uncovering the nuances that make this city unique. By experiencing the city through a local's eyes, you'll find hidden gems, scenic spots, and the best times to avoid crowds at popular attractions. From the rhythm of local markets to the charm of quiet alleys, here's a guide to experiencing Mumbai in a deeper, more authentic way.

Mumbai Through a Local's Eyes: Authentic Experiences and Hidden Gems

Mumbai is a city of contrasts, where modernity meets tradition, and skyscrapers rise alongside centuries-old temples. Locals know the quieter spots and under-the-radar experiences that capture Mumbai's authentic essence. Here are a few insider favorites:

1. Worli Village

    For a true glimpse into Mumbai's fishing heritage, head to Worli Village. Nestled beside the iconic Worli Sea Link, this centuries-old fishing hamlet stands in stark contrast to the surrounding cityscape. Stroll through the narrow lanes to see colorful fishing boats, bustling fish markets, and traditional homes. Visit in the early morning to watch the fishermen bring in their daily catch—a timeless ritual that shows Mumbai's connection to the sea.

2. Khotachiwadi
    This historic village in Girgaon is one of Mumbai's last remaining East Indian enclaves. Known for its charming Portuguese-style cottages and narrow lanes, Khotachiwadi feels worlds away from Mumbai's high-rises and traffic.

Wander through this neighborhood to experience the city's colonial past and interact with locals who have preserved their culture and heritage through generations. Photographers will love the pastel-colored houses, ornate balconies, and the unique blend of Indian and Portuguese architecture.

3. Mahalaxmi Dhobi Ghat

    A truly unique attraction, the Mahalaxmi Dhobi Ghat is the world's largest open-air laundromat, where thousands of washermen, or "dhobis," scrub clothes daily. Visiting here offers an insight into a profession and community that has been an integral part of Mumbai's social fabric for generations. Arrive early in the morning to watch the dhobis at work in an organized, rhythmic process. It's an unfiltered look at Mumbai's industrial spirit and provides some incredible photo opportunities.

4. Bandra Art District

    Known for its vibrant street art, the Bandra Art District, particularly around Chapel Road and Ranwar Village, is a hub for creativity. Explore these winding streets to find colorful murals and graffiti, often themed around social issues, Bollywood icons, or Mumbai's diverse culture. This area draws artists from across India, and new pieces frequently appear, making every visit unique.

Best Photo Spots: Capturing Mumbai's Scenic and Vibrant Moments

From historic landmarks to bustling markets and serene coastlines, Mumbai offers countless photo-worthy locations. Whether you're an avid photographer or a casual visitor looking to capture memories, these spots will bring out the best of Mumbai's energy and beauty.

1. Gateway of India at Sunrise

   The Gateway of India, one of Mumbai's most iconic landmarks, is best visited at sunrise. Early mornings offer a calm, quiet ambiance, with the first rays illuminating the structure in a warm golden light. This is also an ideal time to capture the structure without large crowds. Walk along the nearby promenade for views of the Taj Mahal Palace Hotel and the harbor.

2. Marine Drive at Sunset

   Also known as the Queen's Necklace, Marine Drive is a top spot for sunset photography. As the sun sets, the entire promenade lights up, creating a picturesque contrast between the city's skyline and the Arabian Sea. Capture long-exposure shots of the traffic lights for an urban feel, or focus on the dramatic colors of the sky reflected on the water. You'll find locals and tourists alike gathering to enjoy the views, adding a lively atmosphere to your photos.

3. Haji Ali Dargah

   Located on a small islet in the Arabian Sea, Haji Ali Dargah offers an almost otherworldly scene, especially at high tide. Capture the dargah from the walkway leading up to it, as the waves crash against the path. The combination of the mosque's white architecture against the blue sea makes for a stunning, serene shot. For the best lighting, plan your visit either early in the morning or just before sunset.

4. Sanjay Gandhi National Park

   This green oasis offers a striking contrast to Mumbai's urban landscape, and it's ideal for nature photography. Inside, you'll find the ancient Kanheri Caves, lush forests, and a variety of wildlife. Go early in the morning to capture misty views over the trees and catch a glimpse of the park's resident deer or rare birds.

Timing Your Visit: When to Avoid Crowds, Best Times for Attractions

Mumbai is bustling at almost any hour, but timing can make a difference in the quality of your experience, especially if you're looking to avoid large crowds and long lines. Here's how to make the most of your visit by timing your day wisely.

1. Early Mornings for Popular Attractions

    Attractions like the Gateway of India, Marine Drive, and even the bustling Crawford Market are best visited early in the morning, around 7–8 AM. Not only are crowds thinner, but the cooler morning air makes for a more pleasant experience, especially during Mumbai's warmer months. You'll also have a better chance to interact with locals or shopkeepers preparing for the day.

2. Off-Peak Season

    If you're looking to avoid crowds altogether, the best time to visit Mumbai is during the monsoon months from June to September, when tourist numbers are lower. Although there are heavier rains, you'll experience a less crowded city, and accommodation prices are often reduced. Alternatively, November through February is ideal for pleasant weather, but expect higher visitor numbers during this peak season.

3. Weekday Visits to Markets and Shopping Areas

    Mumbai's local markets like Crawford Market, Chor Bazaar, and Colaba Causeway are always busy, but weekdays offer a slightly more relaxed experience compared to weekends. Aim for a mid-morning visit on a weekday, around 11 AM, when vendors are set up and crowds are manageable. This timing also allows for more meaningful interactions with shopkeepers, who are less rushed than they might be on weekends.

4. Festivals and Cultural Events

   Mumbai celebrates a number of festivals that offer a fantastic glimpse into its cultural vibrancy, but these can also draw large crowds. Major festivals like Ganesh Chaturthi in August or September and Diwali in October or November bring the city alive with decorations, processions, and celebrations. If you prefer a quieter experience, plan your visit around these festivals. However, if you're keen to immerse yourself in Mumbai's culture, visiting during these times can be unforgettable—just expect bustling crowds and vibrant energy.

Visiting Mumbai with a local's perspective allows you to experience more than just its popular sights. It's about discovering the spirit of the city in its lesser-known corners, early-morning calm, and hidden alleys full of history and creativity. By following these insider tips and capturing Mumbai through unique photo spots and well-timed visits, you'll gain a deeper appreciation of this dynamic city that constantly balances old and new, peace and bustle, tradition and modernity. Each moment you spend here will reveal a little more of Mumbai's magic, leaving you with lasting memories of a city that's as diverse as it is unforgettable.

MUMBAI TRAVEL GUIDE 2025

Conclusion

As your journey through the vibrant city of Mumbai draws to a close, it's essential to leave equipped with practical knowledge and resources that ensure a safe, enjoyable, and enriching experience. This conclusion will provide you with useful contacts for emergencies and essential services, as well as insights into Mumbai's seasonal weather and packing tips to make your trip as comfortable as possible.

Useful Contacts: Emergency Numbers, Consulates, and Travel Agencies

Mumbai is a bustling metropolis, and while it offers a wealth of experiences, being prepared for any situation is vital. Below is a list of essential contacts to keep at hand during your visit.

1. Emergency Numbers

    o   Police: 100

    o   Ambulance: 102

    o   Fire Department: 101

    o   Disaster Management: 108
        These numbers are crucial for accessing immediate assistance in case of emergencies. Mumbai's police and medical services operate 24/7, ensuring help is always available.

2. Consulates and Embassies

If you require assistance related to visas, lost documents, or emergencies, knowing the contact information for your country's embassy or consulate can be invaluable. Here are a few key locations:

- United States Consulate General

  Address: 78, Bhulabhai Desai Road, Mumbai - 400026
  Phone: +91 22 2672 4000

- British Deputy High Commission

  Address: 20, Mount Road, Cuffe Parade, Mumbai - 400005
  Phone: +91 22 6650 2000

- Canadian Consulate General

  Address: 100, Marine Drive, Mumbai - 400020
  Phone: +91 22 6748 3000
  Always check the latest contact information and services offered before your trip, as this can vary by location.

3. Travel Agencies

   While navigating Mumbai independently can be rewarding, travel agencies can assist with logistics, guided tours, and local insights. Consider these reputable agencies:

   - Thomas Cook India
   - MakeMyTrip
   - SOTC Travel
     Each of these agencies offers various services, including customizable travel packages, hotel bookings, and guided tours that can enhance your Mumbai experience.

Mumbai by Season: Weather Guide and Packing Tips

Mumbai's tropical climate means that the weather varies significantly throughout the year. Understanding the seasons will help you pack appropriately and plan your activities.

1. Winter (November to February)

    o   Weather: Mild and pleasant, with temperatures ranging from 15°C to 30°C (59°F to 86°F). Humidity levels are also lower, making it a comfortable time for outdoor activities.

    o   Packing Tips: Bring light layers, as evenings can get cool. Comfortable shoes are essential for walking around, and don't forget a hat and sunglasses to protect against the sun.

2. Summer (March to May)

    o   Weather: Hot and humid, with temperatures often exceeding 35°C (95°F). The city can feel stifling, especially in April and May.

    o   Packing Tips: Lightweight, breathable clothing is key. Opt for cotton or linen fabrics that wick moisture. A good sunscreen is crucial, and always stay hydrated. Consider carrying a reusable water bottle to refill as you explore.

3. Monsoon (June to September)

    o   Weather: Characterized by heavy rainfall and high humidity, the monsoon season can bring occasional flooding and transportation disruptions. Temperatures range from 24°C to 30°C (75°F to 86°F).

    o   Packing Tips: Waterproof clothing, including a lightweight raincoat and waterproof footwear, will keep you dry. An umbrella is also useful. Plan indoor activities on days with heavy rain, and check weather forecasts regularly to avoid travel disruptions.

4. Post-Monsoon (October)

    o   Weather: The weather begins to cool slightly, and the humidity decreases, making it a comfortable time to visit. Temperatures range from 24°C to 32°C (75°F to 90°F).

    o   Packing Tips: Light layers will work well during this transitional period. It's an excellent time for outdoor sightseeing, so comfortable shoes and sun protection remain essential.

As you conclude your travel preparations, keep these practical tips in mind to ensure a seamless experience in Mumbai. By being informed about emergency contacts, understanding the city's seasonal changes, and packing appropriately, you're setting yourself up for a rewarding adventure. Mumbai is a city full of life, culture, and unforgettable experiences, and with the right preparation, you'll be able to immerse yourself in all it has to offer. Safe travels!

Printed in Dunstable, United Kingdom